Wot, No School?

How schools impede education

Jonathan Langdale and John Harrison

Illustrations by Laura Davey

How schools impede education

Published by
Best Global Publishing
PO Box 9366
Brentwood
Essex CM13 1ZT
United Kingdom

First published 2007
Second edition 2009

A record of this book is in the British Library

http://www.bestglobalpublishing.com

The Purpose of this Book

The purpose of this book is to start a debate about the *real* problem of how we should educate our young people. To be winners today, young people have to be 'good at school' (or very lucky). A great many of them – about half – aren't 'good at school' and are thus classed as failures before life has properly begun.

We believe that *all* are good at *something*.

The great barrier to education for teachers and learners is the system; the institution of school itself (especially post fourteen) and the ludicrous insistence that *academic ability is the greatest good* for all young people. This strange notion is based on nothing more than the fact that schools have *always* taught academic subjects and learners have *always* been measured by their academic ability. Those who are successful at this go on, in their time, to control the institutional school industry – and what was good enough for them...

Now we measure the 'performance of schools' (as if inanimate institutions can 'perform') so that teachers and heads can be rewarded or castigated and the institution treated like a manufacturing production line processing identical raw materials and trying to produce identical 'outputs'. Schools and the industry that controls them – from government to quangos to local authorities to Ofsted and now to something new to control 'academies' – have become more important than the unique individual human beings that they try to process.

How schools impede education

No one has stopped to ask 'What is education *for*?' Instead, they go on measuring the measurable – academic attainments – and ignoring the nurture of non-academic abilities and of what cannot be measured: independence of thought, originality and creativity, sociability, willingness to co-operate with others, a 'can do' autonomous approach to life and so on. These are the very birthright of every young person regardless of her or his academic ability.

This book reveals how modern Britain arrived at this present fixation with academic success and proposes a radical approach to the business of educating our young people to ensure that *all* will have the opportunity both to take a full and positive part in adult life and to develop their own peculiar and particular sets of aptitudes and abilities.

Join the debate by visiting www.wotnoschool.com the website that is dedicated to debating the issues addressed in this book

Contents

How schools impede education

Wot, No School?

Acknowledgements

This is not an academic work, but we have sought the advice of a number of professional academics, teachers and heads and what stands out is the sheer *kindness* that we were shown, whether in reading and commenting on the many early drafts or in prolonged telephone conversations, suggestions as to further reading, references or forwarding of academic papers. In particular we were much encouraged by Professors Charles Handy, Robert Fisher, John Radford, James Tooley, Alison Wolf, Vivian Hill and John Howson. We must also thank the members of Skill Force Ltd. for allowing us to sit in on their work with young students in Sittingbourne, the FE Colleges who feature in the book and Ann Cockerham and the staff and pupils of Thomas Peacock School in Rye (now Rye Community College).

Despite the frustrations of government websites, 0845 numbers and the dense thickets of bureaucracy, there some (many) extremely nice and helpful civil servants once you find them. Dave Walton and Jessica Vince of the DfES (now called something else with no mention of education) are a representative sample of the several in that department and elsewhere who were unfailingly pleasant, patient and helpful to amateur researchers such as we.

[For the second edition I am indebted to the critical oversight of Alan Gorman, and for the thoughtful suggestions of others, particularly Paula Berry and David Stone who have read the first edition. I must pay a special tribute to Laura Davey (aged 14) for drawing the cartoons that enliven the text.   J.H.]

How schools impede education

Wot, No School?

Jonathan Langdale 1941 – 2006

Jonathan Langdale died on Christmas Eve 2006 of a nasty and virulent cancer that had progressed rapidly though the year, shortly before this book first went to print.

I sorely miss his collaboration, friendship and good humour. I shall as sorely miss his help in carrying the debate on education forward but, thankfully, the issue itself is greater than the pair of us together could ever make it. It stands on its own merits and will be carried forward by minds possibly as incisive as his, though I doubt with greater passion.

J. H.
February 2009

How schools impede education

Wot, No School?

An education ought to be very good, to justify depriving a child of its liberty.

J. S. Mill (*attrib.*)

How schools impede education

Wot, No School?

Chapter One

What is Education for?

Less than half of school leavers gain five GCSEs including English and Maths at grade C or above.

Does this mean that more than half are failures?

Or are we failing them?

Generalisation 1

"The trouble is we're producing school leavers who don't know right from wrong, don't know how to behave, many of them can't read and write or do simple arithmetic and some, according to a recent news report, can't even speak clearly."

True? Well, the measured facts are that in England:

- just under 30% of students do well at school – i.e. they achieve three or more A-levels or equivalent [1]
- getting on for another 20% achieve the government's desired objective for school success (5 A*-C grades at GCSE including English and maths)

How schools impede education

"...don't know right from wrong ...can't even speak clearly."

- around 30% of students (or 218,117) managed to get between one and four grades A*-C at GCSE [2]
- another 20% or so (120,744) got less than that, but managed at least one grade A*-G [2]
- 1.1% failed to get any kind of grade: that is 7,141 to the nearest whole student.[2]

[[1] Source: National Statistics DCSF GCE/VCE A/AS and Equivalent Examination Results in England 2006/2007 (Revised), Reference SFR 02/2008, Figure 1: Time Series of GCE/VCE/Applied A-level (or equivalent) achievement of 17 year-olds
[2] Source: National Statistics, DCFS reference SFR 01/2008, Table 6: GCSE and equivalent attempts and achievements of pupils at the end of Key Stage 4. 2006/2007 revised, England.]

Wot, No School?

Generalisations 2, 3 and 4

"Young people have always behaved badly and got into trouble."

"The confusing thing is that they are the apples of their mothers' eyes and can behave quite well a lot of the time."

"In fact, they can be shockingly kind on occasions."

Besides, what do the measured facts really tell us? What are these GCSEs and A-levels (or equivalent)? Who chooses the curriculum? Who sets the exams? Who decides what is a Grade A*? Why did they invent a Grade A*? Was it because too many people were getting a Grade A? (Answer: yes) So were the exams getting easier or are the candidates all getting cleverer? Or are the teachers getting better at getting them through the exams?

In any case, even if the number of students getting five 'good' GCSEs has improved by five or six per cent since the year 2000, that still leaves around fifty per cent without that magic number. Are they to be written off as failures?

Above all, does 5 Grade A*-C GCSEs represent an education?

Everyone from academics and educationalists to parents and ordinary people argue about it. It's all very confusing, so let's look at the problem another way.

How schools impede education

If you were an employer, what general qualities (i.e. not job-specific skills) would you be looking for in a young employee?

We've asked that question of various groups when talking to them about education and we get roughly the same list:

- Read and write
- Add up and subtract
- Honesty, integrity
- Wanting to do a good job
- Punctuality
- Desire to learn
- Work in a team
- Loyalty
- Good manners
- Commitment
- Initiative
- Responsibility
- Enquiring mind
- Self presentation
- Energy

Generally, they want people who can read and write and do simple arithmetic, have an agreeable manner and can get on well with others, can make themselves understood clearly (either directly or on the telephone), can ask relevant questions to reveal or clarify other people's needs, show initiative when necessary and, above all, be honest and reliable.

Wot, No School?

We've never heard them say they want a minimum GCSE Grade C in English or Maths or French or Geography… or any other academic qualification.

Nevertheless, in spite of being apparently uninterested in academic results, employers do still want to see them on candidates' CVs. Why is that? Well, interviewing applicants for a job vacancy is a time-consuming and very expensive activity. Employers, especially those in small and medium sized companies, don't have time to interview every applicant. Although they are aware that they may be missing a really good candidate this way, many use academic qualifications as a rough filter to reduce the list to a manageable number.

That's about as far as their interest in academic qualifications runs. Of course, politics and political posturing come into play a lot here. The government sets great store by academic qualifications and how important they are for the 'highly skilled' employment world. This enables think tanks of a different political colour to point up the government failings in 'improving' educational outcomes. The Bow Group worked out that 'approaching one million' pupils left school between 1997 and 2008 without five GCSE grade Gs including English and maths and that pupils without five GCSE C grades risked "becoming unemployable".
[The Failed Generation: The Real Cost of Education under Labour 2008]

The "unemployable" quotation was based on a 2006 survey by the Learning and Skills Council which found that 22 per cent of employers would not recruit pupils without these grades. That sounds terrible… until you read further on that 74 per cent of employers in the same survey said they *would* do so – although they qualified this by saying that they would "only offer unskilled positions with low pay and limited prospects". [LSC News Release, publication number 379 – GCSE Drop-Outs 'Unemployable'] A 2006 report for the Confederation of British Industry also found that 'only 54.5 per cent of employers' set minimum levels of qualifications for new recruits, though what these are was not specified. [Working on the Three Rs – Employers' Priorities for Functional Skills in Maths and English]

All we can conclude from this, then, is that it may be *harder* but it is by no means *impossible* to find employment when you leave school without five 'good' GCSEs. An unskilled job with low pay and limited prospects is still a job, and being in full time employment is a big addition to your CV, especially if it carries with it a reference to your honesty, reliability and so on.

Here's a list of what most of the people we've talked to want in a school leaver compared with the statutory curriculum subjects they are taught at school. Column A is the list of what they are looking for. Column B is the official list of what schools try to give our young people, with varying degrees of success (the compulsory curriculum).

A. What they want	B. What they get
Read and write	English
Add up and subtract	Mathematics
Honesty, integrity	Science
Wanting to do a good job	Technology
Punctuality	History

Wot, No School?

Desire to learn
Work in a team
Loyalty
Good manners
Commitment
Initiative
Responsibility
Enquiring mind
Self presentation
Energy

Geography
A foreign language
Art
Music
Physical exercise

Actually, of course, they don't only want the things in Column A and schools don't only give them the things in Column B. One may be sure that employers would have no problem with school leavers having a knowledge and appreciation of art and music or with being physically fit. So we need to refine both lists. In any case, education is not just for the benefit of future employers; *it must primarily be for the welfare and quality of life of the student.*

In short, young people need not only to be able to cope with the modern world, but to grow with and benefit from the many things it has to offer.

They need to be able to find their way from A to B, using public transport and a timetable as well as being able to find it out on the web (not everyone has a Blackberry yet). And be able to ask directions politely if they are not sure.

How schools impede education

"This boy does well to find his way home at night."
- the late teacher and radio panellist, Arthur Marshall's
geography report on one of his students.

They need to be able to understand what is meant by 'gross', 'net' and 'APR' when it comes to saving money or using a credit card; what a mortgage is and an overdraft; what insurance is in its many different forms.

They need to know how to use domestic appliances safely and efficiently. That may mean learning something about the nature of electricity and gas and why they should be treated with respect.

They need to be aware of the environment, how the human race has affected it and the implications this has for climate change.

Wot, No School?

They need to be able to write letters – covering letters, letters of congratulation, letters of thanks, letters of complaint and so on.

They need to be able to fill in a myriad government and local government forms and also forms at work. Maybe they need to try designing forms… After all, someone needs to improve the forms we're all obliged to fill in.

They need to be able to describe something they have seen or would like to do or would like to see happen both verbally and in writing, but in either case clearly and interestingly. At work they would, perhaps, need to be able to write an accident report that must be precise and coherent.

They need to know something about the law of the land and what their rights and responsibilities are as citizens.

They need to know about the great religions of the world and be able to compare one with another and with non-religious world views.

A full list of our suggestions for the 'school' stage of education is given in Chapter 6.

This short book is intended to get you to develop a debate about:

- The things that young people need to know and be able to do as they stand on the threshold of adulthood – around 14 or 15 years old for most of them

How schools impede education

- The range of opportunities they should be afforded to help develop their many and various aptitudes and abilities
- Why these major changes to our education system are necessary
- How all this might be accomplished

Apart from analysing how we arrived at the system of schooling we have at present and why it is failing a significant percentage of our young people, the book will propose some pretty radical solutions that challenge the underlying assumptions and received wisdom on which the whole edifice rests. That is why the call for change needs to come, not from government, not from quangos or educationalists, but from parents, from employers, from teachers, from young people themselves – anyone, in fact, who is not part of the ruling educational establishment and therefore doesn't have a vested interest in maintaining the status quo.

This book is not an attack on teachers. They are the bedrock on which the proposals stand. The number of teachers we have spoken to (and there are many dozens so far) who, once we explained the ideas, reject them, may be counted on the fingers of one hand. The vast majority are very enthusiastic.

We do not pretend that this book has all the solutions or that those proposed cannot be improved upon. That is why a debate is needed. Collectively we are much more likely to come up with workable and successful solutions. We must work out and explain the details clearly and gain widespread acceptance and support before anything as big and complex as these changes can be successfully implemented. To that end, there is a website: www.wotnoschool.com with a forum page on which your ideas and thoughts may be posted. Emails may be sent to debate@wotnoschool.com

Chapter Two

What's the Problem?

'People rarely just fail to learn; they leave us with the problem of finding out what it was they were learning while they were not learning what we expected them to learn.'
Salmon and Bannister *Education for Teaching* 1974

We are all of us different. We are different shapes and sizes; we have different metabolic rates; we come from different home backgrounds – some wealthy, most middling, some poor, some harmonious, some very difficult; we live in different places, in different neighbourhoods and so on. We also like different things; we are better at some things than we are at others – no one is good at everything and everyone can be good at something, given the right help and the right opportunity. As young people, we have different aptitudes – which we shall define narrowly as the *capacity* to acquire or develop a particular skill to a better than average degree. That doesn't mean we cannot all develop *some* ability in any activity or that, by practising and being coached, we cannot improve our performance in any area. (When Admiral Lord Nelson lost his right arm, he became quite good at writing with his left hand.) We simply mean that our levels of ability in any given activity will vary enormously. By 'skill' and 'activity' we don't just mean physical skills; they include every activity undertaken by the human race from laying a brick to throwing a javelin to translating the Greek philosophers to nuclear physics. Those with aptitude in any area seem to have a natural tendency, propensity or disposition for that activity – a talent one could say.

How is it that 'education' has been narrowed down from developing in young people those multifarious talents or aptitudes that they possess as individuals, to the list of compulsory curriculum subjects listed in Chapter One?

The first thing we have to do is to recognise that 'education' and 'school' are *not* synonymous terms. This may sound like a statement of the bleedin' obvious, but there is a common assumption that education takes place in schools and therefore if we improve schools, we improve education. And *that*, as the statistics showed in Chapter One, is manifestly not the case.

It isn't the teachers who are getting education wrong. It isn't the pupils who can't learn. It isn't the parents who make the wrong choice… It's the system: the ludicrous insistence that *academic ability is the greatest good* for all children whatever their individual aptitudes and preferences, despite the fact that once you have left school almost no-one is remotely interested in your *academic* ability – except, perhaps, another academic institution.

The solution isn't *more choice*, it isn't *better schools*. It's *different education*.

The solution proposed in this book is based on asking what is *education* for? Rather than what are *schools* for? It is based on a consideration of what learners and teachers need rather than what institutions and bureaucrats need. We will ask two simple questions:

- What are our children learning?
- Why are they learning it?

Education and School

Throughout time the primary function of 'education' has been the transmission of the values and the accumulated knowledge of a society from one generation to another.

The primary function of 'school', particularly secondary school, in our century is not so clear. Is its function to teach values and knowledge, or skills and techniques? If so, whose values? What knowledge? Which skills? To which pupils?

Is 'school' there to instruct pupils in right behaviour and attitudes, the best way to get on in life, to win friends and influence people – or to train them in carrying out the functions they will need to carry out in adult life – the 'real' world as we tell the boys and girls (rather than the imaginary, 'virtual reality' one, which is a school)?

Is it there to discover their talents, release their creativity, teach them how to think?

Is the function of a school to do all of these things? And, is it to do all these things for all pupils at the same time and at the same age: or at the time and at the age which is most fruitful for them as individuals?

Wot, No School?

How many of these functions are compatible? In how many of them, and for how many pupils, do schools, **can** schools succeed?

In short – do schools provide positive benefits for the majority of those who pass through them; are they the best way of achieving what we want to achieve for all our young people; do they give everyone the best chance; *could our society do as well or better without them*?

After all, the 1944 Education Act states that the parent of every school-age child should ensure that he or she receives full-time education suitable to his or her age and ability "either by regular attendance at school *or otherwise*". (Our italics)

Education

Education throughout time and throughout all societies has been focussed upon guiding our behaviour towards the adult ways of the culture into which we have been born and towards the roles we will eventually play within it. In its fullest form education means the drawing out and development of all mental and physical skills and aptitudes, for the benefit of individuals as well as society.

Once we have become adults we all play a part in educating, for good or ill, the next generation. We do this as parents, grandparents, managers, leaders, employers, writers, artists, role models, exemplars, heroes, villains, criminals, preachers, and presenters...

How schools impede education

Schools and school teachers represent only a specialised part of that education.

Education ain't only books and music - it's asking questions all the time.
[Beattie Bryant in Arnold Wesker's 'Roots']

Does our school system encourage teachers and pupils to ask questions all the time – or is it required to supply answers?

The man stood in front of the class. 'Now learn this he said', writing an equation on the board. We wrote it in our books. Three months later we wrote it out again in an examination paper. If the second time of writing was the same as the first, we had learnt it. I exaggerate, but only a little…Later on I came to realise that I had learned nothing at school which I now remember except only this – that all problems had already been solved, by someone, and that the answer was around, in the back of the book or the teachers' head. Learning seemed to mean transferring answers from them to me.
Charles Handy *The Age of Unreason 1990*

Why is the world full of brilliant children and dud grown-ups?
G.K.Chesterton

Needs careful watching since he borders on the brilliant.
Report to Army promotions board

Wot, No School?

What part does our school system play in a 'negative education' process, schooling bright, enquiring children into successful givers of 'right' answers, and making most of us highly suspicious in adult life of anyone who isn't good at following the prescribed pathways we learned at school? Is that what 'education' is about?

On the one hand we need to be clear about what we mean by education and what we think it is for: on the other hand we need to know what we think our schools are for.

Schools

What do learners need?

- Guidance as to how to learn
- The tools for independent learning
- Ownership of meaningful knowledge
- Optimism – the knowledge that they have a real chance to succeed
- Hope – based on the experience of previous success
- The expectation of success
- Encouragement to success – praise
- Motivating, empathetic teachers
- Wise, skilled and knowledgeable teachers
- The creation of the best conditions for learning
- Permission to fail
- Good reasons for trying again *"Defeat is not important. It is how you come back from defeat that is important"* Sir Alex Ferguson.

How schools impede education

How do 'schools' with their need for order, for managers, for convincing external Authorities they have met institutional targets in order to be given the money to do what the Authority wants, help with these things?

How do 'schools' hinder these learners and their teachers?

Schools are, of necessity, concerned with *what* we learn and have made themselves expert in selecting and organising the 'subjects' they will teach so that their 'output' of examinations passed and grades achieved will be approved and rewarded by their paymasters – the Government. Being measured for how they teach young people to *think* and *learn* is much more difficult, so it is simply ignored by the authorities and teachers are not rewarded for this crucial responsibility.

How did schools get the way they are? Where are they now? Where are they going?

What are they *for*?

There follows a brief, thumbnail sketch of the developments of Western education, which explains how we arrived at the curriculum and the attitudes towards 'education' and 'school' we now have. If you already know all about that, or don't think it's important at this point, skip this section and go on to Chapter Three.

Wot, No School?

*

A Potted Nutshell History of What Went Wrong

In the earliest societies the environment in which you lived and the things you had to do to survive in that environment were your 'school', your fellow survivors were your 'classes' and many, probably most adults were your 'teachers'. In these societies children became both participators and learners. Their learning, as Margaret Mead, the American anthropologist described it, was based on empathy, identification and imitation.

More complex societies began to acquire a body of knowledge which was greater than one person could know. Children needed to be formally initiated into the adult world, if they were to play a full part in it. They needed to know more than their parents individually knew. In societies which were still mainly nomadic they were given a period of time, usually in a secluded place with a few selected adults, in which they could be taught the cultural values, the past experiences, the myths, the rituals and the religious beliefs of their society. These were mainly imparted by older men with specialist knowledge in these areas.

After the development of the settled town, new specialist skills and knowledge and ways of living developed. There was more to be learned than could be understood by doing and imitating. More learning could be abstracted from practice, learned out of the working context, from adults who had distilled the experience and knowledge of the society, than could be gained from

How schools impede education

simply observing and imitating the work of parents or other individuals.

Specialist organisations responded to the special needs of special groups of people in a particular society. One of the first impulses came from religion, which relied on the arcane skills and knowledge of priests or shamans for its effect and power. Only those who were 'chosen' could serve the god and present the god to the people. Priests passed their knowledge on secretly to the 'chosen ones', taught and trained in special groups, in 'schools'.

The discovery first of reckoning and recording and then writing, as a means of passing on knowledge and information from one person to another, conferred power on those who could do it. They weren't skills that anyone could acquire simply by imitation, watching what somebody else did and copying it, or learned by simply memorising what you had seen or heard. Intellectual, abstract ideas, theories needed to be learned and understood, so they needed to be taught by those who understood them - and learned by those who had time to learn them.

The word 'school' is derived from the Greek 'skolē' meaning leisure. Schools and the learning they transmitted were originally reserved for the children, especially the sons, of the wealthy, who didn't need to work. It was considered that for the daughters there was enough to be done in the hazardous business of giving birth to and rearing children, let alone in running a household to at least the standards set by her mother as well as those expected by her husband, to give her little or no 'skolē' at all.

Wot, No School?

Consequently the learning was tailored to the various requirements of the wealthy, male, ruling classes or the priesthood, centring around literature – tales of exemplar figures from the past - ideas and theories of number, geometry, algebra; mythology and science; medicine; sport and military tactics and techniques; philosophy, public speaking, logical argument and debate; aesthetics such as music, drama, poetry; morality, including politics (yes, politics and morality were once believed to be contiguous!) sensitivity and duty towards people and monarch or state; and/or theories about the management of estates, money and the workers; all as either the pursuit of knowledge for its own sake, or as the management of that particular society, or the dominance of its religion demanded.

Hence the academic approach to schooling. The theoretical study of the arts and sciences, suitable for those who belonged to the wealthy, ruling classes who had the time, leisure and slaves of one kind or another to do the work for them, has persisted to this day – for those who don't.

The medieval foundation of education in English schools was an adherence to "Christ, King Henrie, the boke and the bowe". The Church exercised a strong grip on education - almost all teaching and learning was in Latin - and the Universities concentrated on Literae Humaniores, which they continued well into the 20th century. As the affluence and power of the state grew and the 'knightly' classes were superseded by the expansionist and mercantile spirit of the times, the chess and lute playing education of those who would make verses, respect the rules of courtesy and the knightly exercises of chivalries of war fell away, too. Most boys

How schools impede education

(and a few of their sisters, at least at the elementary stages) learned from a private tutor at home, though an increasing number were sent to the emerging, fee-paying Public Schools, which took as their models the educational ideas of Athens and Rome. After a while they returned to the notion of taking boys away as boarders to a secluded place with a few selected adults, in which they could be taught the cultural values, the past experiences, the myths, the rituals and the religious beliefs of their society.

They taught them Latin and Greek (the wisdom of the golden times), the Bible, a little English literature which was deemed worthy of comparison with the great classical authors, some history, particularly military and political, the geography of the empire, mathematical theories (with geometry being particularly useful for those who would rule the waves or bring the guns to bear), sport – *mens sana in corpore sano* – and service to God and monarch. They were preparing their scions to rule their lands and their workers, for the Church the Law and the Army, to serve King and Country under the laws of God, to die in the sunlight outside an Indian fort helping to build an empire which would bring the right ideas, the right beliefs, the right knowledge and the right values to a world which had not previously had the privilege.

Lagging only slightly behind the original schools for the sons of the leisured classes, came the 'scribe' schools, developing an administrative class, to serve the aristocracy, the military and the priesthood. Originating in Egypt and Mesopotamia they first taught reading and writing in 'school' groups, then gave pupils, from the age of about 13 or 14, practical training, often through an apprenticeship system, in the various offices for which they were being prepared. They were popular and much sought after schools, for alumni were pretty well guaranteed escape from hard manual labour, a lucrative job for life and access to considerable power and privilege.

Medieval England provided something similar, through monastic schools which taught boys from the higher social orders, below the ranks of the aristocracy, elementary literacy, some Latin, perhaps a little Greek, but also arithmetic, geometry, astronomy, and physics, qualifying them to enter the monastery at about 15 with the same advantages as those enjoyed by the former pupils of the 'scribe' schools. Later, education was extended to artisan boys, elementary reading and writing and arithmetic, to enable them to join their trades and guilds.

A little later still, alongside the emergence of the Public Schools for the ruling classes, came the grammar schools, day schools for the sons of the merchants and local dignitaries, often founded by the new men who had made their wealth by trade or in the City, without benefit of the refined education of the aristocracy, and who aspired for more for the succeeding generations. Following the only model that existed these, too, were built on the notion that academic excellence, the ability to study the theories and ideas of the arts and sciences, rather than to apply them in any practical fashion, was the greatest good. They were based on the same classical foundation, geared a little differently to reflect the social status and future activities of their pupils. Hence, Shakespeare, who attended a grammar school, could be referred to by a member of the aristocracy of the time as

How schools impede education

having 'small Latin and less Greek', though the Latin and Greek he did possess would probably have made entry to read Classics at a modern university no problem.

The requirements of education, the knowledge and values to be passed on to the ruling and the wealth-creating classes, changed only slowly for boys in the centuries after Shakespeare. Science, sparked into life by the excitements of the Renaissance, and modern foreign languages, especially French and Italian, grew in importance; a few more girls learned a little more than those things required to capture a husband, run a household, work in a shop or on a farm and rear the future generation. Aristocratic girls learned such things as music, painting, drawing, a little French or Italian, but nothing 'heavy' like Latin or Greek, or mathematics or science or philosophy, on the grounds that their minds were too delicately constructed to tackle such strenuous activity. The daughters of lawyers, doctors, bankers and the rising mercantile classes were encouraged to do likewise in order to raise their social status and 'marriage-ability', not in order to become anything so vulgar as a musician or painter or writer.

In the nineteenth century things began to progress more rapidly. Church-run Sunday Schools had already started to teach Bible reading to both boys and girls from the less privileged classes. At the beginning of the century Parliament passed the Health and Morals for Apprentices Act. Starting as they were to go on, the politicians decided that employers should enable apprentices to learn basic mathematics as well as reading and writing. Pleased with this benevolent idea they did nothing further about it, and life went on much the same as before. However a number of outcries from writers and

Wot, No School?

reformers, appalled by the conditions of the under-privileged classes and by the Dotheboys Halls of the times, stirred Parliament into further activity. In 1870 the Elementary Education Act was passed, demanding a basic education (though not schooling) in the three R's for all. It was not until 1880 that it was compulsory throughout England and Wales.

However, secondary and higher education remained voluntary, whether privately with a tutor at home or in a Public School, a grammar school or a University. Though scholarships to pay the cost of tuition were available for some academically very able boys (and some girls, too), school was, in reality, only accessible to those families who could afford both the fees and the absence of earning power of their children. They remained an option for the social and intellectual elite alone – with an academic, not practical curriculum and a teaching method to suit.

So, just as it has got interesting for those who are interested, the bell has rung. Now we have to go to Chapter Three.

Chapter Three

Up the Institution!

In the 20th century, the politicisation and the inevitable bureaucratisation and centralisation of schooling, gathered steam. A Board of Education (a name to set philanthropic, bureaucratic and political pulses racing) had been established in 1899.

Three years later the Balfour Act introduced local government for both secondary and elementary schooling (though they called it education), and the emergence of the Local Education Authority (hurrah for the triumph of bureaucracy) which had the powers to provide secondary schools and develop technical education (which, of course, soon meant technical schools). This led swiftly on to the Education Act of 1918 which aimed at a "national system of public education available for all persons capable of profiting thereby", with a school leaving age raised to 14, though some Local Education Authorities (LEAs) could extend it to 15.

The next war prompted the next big change, (curious how the end of wars seemed to prompt the government of the day to change what we did in schools – were we already beginning to blame the teachers?) the 1944 Education Act, from which much good came for many people but which, in the tradition of the Law of Unintended Consequences, sowed the seeds of the system which is, sixty five years later, according to the last Prime Minister, "continuing to let down too many children, despite…years of reform and record levels of investment…"

The Butler Act required that the taxpayer should be responsible for the provision of secondary education for all, without the necessity to pay any further fees. Though it did not make secondary *schooling* compulsory, from here on in politicians, bureaucrats and later, following their example, parents, the chattering classes, the liberati, and the media pundits have used the terms 'education' and 'school' as though they were synonymous. As this book will demonstrate, however determinedly, or pig-headedly, political/bureaucratic thinking makes it so, **they are not**!

In an admirable stride forward in the understanding that schools should find some way of attending to the different needs of their pupils, and the recognition that different people have different talents and learn in different ways, Butler not only defined three progressive stages of education – primary, secondary and further – but set up the tripartite system of secondary schools, 'grammar, technical and secondary modern'. Sadly the education/schooling muddle soon took care of the good intentions, at least as far as secondary schools were concerned.

The schools which the political, financial, Church and military leaders, the Lords and Commons knew and understood, were for 'academic' education, for maths and Latin and science and French, so grammar schools, which taught naturally academic children by academic methods, were perceived as first class beacons of quality and hope, while the rest, which taught the vast majority of us who are not naturally academic, were perceived as for the second class, or the 'dud', no-hopers. They were still expected to use academic methods and extol academic success as the greatest good, so the 'no-hopers', who were merely good at practical applications and useful things, had even less chance to succeed and even less hope of doing so.

An opportunity to develop the differing talents and skills needed by a changing world was provided by the technical schools. These potentially admirable institutions, the schools which might have led the majority of us out of the academic morass, were undermined from the beginning, by the dread process known as Selection (or the 11+), as being for those who *couldn't* get into the academic grammar schools rather than for those who *could* learn and do what society increasingly needed to be learned and done. They taught such non-academic things as woodwork and technical drawing – "I didn't get where I am today by learning technical drawing" – and even smaller Latin and even less Greek. They were seen from the beginning as schools for grammar school 'failures', their teachers were seen as teachers who couldn't measure up to the best in the academic profession, and their product was considered at best, second best. In the Law of Self-Fulfilling Prophecy they did exactly what we might have expected – they failed. Now they largely don't exist, having merged into comprehensives or climbed by heroic efforts into the ranks of the grammar school to give less academic pupils a chance to be esteemed for doing as well as they can at what they are not naturally good, or to which they are not naturally inclined.

Wot, No School?

As for the secondaries, given a glossy coat of terminological paint as the secondary 'modern', they were Private Frasered, doomed from the start. Can't make it into the grammar, can't even make it into the tech.? No Latin for the likes of you. Shut you up somewhere with all the other dross, on the edge of town, behind brick walls and iron fences, in ugly old, or equally ugly new buildings. Give you a group of obviously even less academic, therefore third class teachers, to struggle along in an imitation of what the 'good', the 'bright' children are doing down the road (which must be 'good', because 'bright' children do it even though it is patently unsuited to you, your method and style of learning, your talents and capabilities). Tell you to do CSE because you're not good enough to do O level and you're not going on to the passport to success, the 'gold standard', the academic A-level. Push you in there from 8.30 to 3.30 five days a week for 40 weeks in the year and then complain like hell about what comes out four or five years later!

Despite the best efforts of numerous dedicated, committed, highly capable teachers, the <u>*institution*</u> *provided the irremovable label, the* <u>*institution*</u> *defined what you did and what you didn't, and the* <u>*institution*</u> *failed you and failed your teachers.*

At the heart of the separation into Grammar, Technical and Secondary Moderns was a Right Idea. It recognised that people have different aptitudes, talents, skills. Only a small proportion of us are naturally 'academic'. Most have other strengths – creative, technical, organisational, physical... In any successful group it is the range of skills, talents and aptitudes which creates the success and which sustains it.

How schools impede education

Recognising that it is our strengths, rather than our weaknesses, that are the most important things we have to offer is common sense. Gaining the motivation and self-esteem that comes from developing our strengths helps us enormously in addressing our weaknesses, where they might be likely to hold us back.

It is only in the school system that the Grammar pupil is considered the 'best', the others 'worse': it is only at school that we hold up academic ability as being the greatest good – regardless of the fact that, once you have left school, no one is remotely interested in your academic ability, except another academic institution. How many of the readers of this book have ever been asked to show their A-level or GCSE certificates to anyone outside an academic environment?

Had the tripartite system grown from that idea – that it is what people *can do well* that should be developed as far as possible and that it is *success* in the development of abilities that should have parity of esteem – we might have avoided many of the self-inflicted ills currently besetting us. We might have learned that it is what you learn to contribute to society that matters, not the institution in which you learn it. We might have learned that a successful engineer, innovator or wealth creator is at least of equal value to a successful doctor, lawyer or accountant and certainly of greater value than an unsuccessful one! We might have looked for creativity, thought, originality as much in the Technical school and the Secondary Modern as in the Grammar and, who knows, with a greater chance of finding it?

It took twenty years for the recognition to dawn that the grammar schools and the independent Public Schools were going on doing what they had done for five hundred years – providing excellent students for the universities, and serving the other needs of the leaders of the nation, in the Armed Services, the Church, the City, the banks, the professions and the Civil Service, in just the same way and in roughly the same proportion as their forebears, the academies and the scribe schools, had done before them.

It was becoming equally clear that the other two parts of the schooling system were also doing just what they had done before – failing to educate the rest.

Enter Shirley Williams and Circular 10/64 with the new solution, the Comprehensive School. Sweep away the notion of 'failure' by sweeping away Selection, the demon 11+. Pile them all into one school, academics, non-academics, technicals and no-hopers. In this one, brand new institution they can all go on doing what they did before, only in a more socially acceptable way. Don't change the education, change the schooling, change the school.

The politicians of the left loved it. The politicians of the right hated it. They loved and hated it for social reasons, for political reasons, for school reasons – not for educational reasons. After all, the pupils were all being offered equality of opportunity - the opportunity to receive the same schooling, in the same subjects, and to take the same examinations, even if the exams were to be graded so that the non-academic 'thickos' could get some marks, somewhere.

The Treasury loved it. Centralisation meant larger, more cost effective units. 1500 pupils in one school, rather than three schools; 30+ pupils in every class; one set of buildings, one set of administrative and maintenance staff, one purchasing department, the economies of scale; schools could only benefit so education could only benefit.

The bureaucrats loved it. The interests of administrators and union officials, if not the pupils and the parents, were well served by greater centralisation. Larger size units meant *"a reduction in the ability of consumers [the parent and the child] to choose, and an increase in the power of producers [teachers and administrators]... by reducing the power of the parents"*. [From *Free to Choose* by Milton and Rose Friedman 1980, published by Secker and Warburg. Reprinted by permission of the Random House Group Ltd.]

Teachers and parents of a left wing persuasion loved it for social reasons. No more stigmatisation by selection failure, everyone has the chance to develop at their own pace and at the appropriate stage of development, to make their way up the school ladder at any time, not just at 11: teachers have the whole range of academic ability to teach, not just the 'second-raters' or the 'duds'. The 'bright' academic child can be given a dose of social reality, while at the same time hauling up the less 'bright' by their academic bootstraps. No more noses will turned up at a different uniform, or entry through different gates. One size fitting all, the school becomes a more accurate reflection of the 'real' world, therefore a better school, therefore delivers a better education.

Pupils did what they usually do, saw through the artificial social engineering, quickly established who was 'good at school' and therefore destined for success in adult life, and who wasn't, shrugged their shoulders and got on with it. The academically 'bright' ones did just as well, or not noticeably worse than they had done before. Of the rest, most of the 'survivors' continued to survive. The 'losers' established early on that what was called 'education' was, as the Elton Report (1989) described it, 'unwinnable' and went on losing.

By 1968 it clearly still wasn't doing what we wanted it to do, so another solution arrived. Some twenty years before, we had made them all stay on at school until they were 15. Now let's make them all stay on until they're 16! Give them another year of the same stuff! That'll work!

Won't it?

Of course, it won't.

Employers saw that it made little difference and continued to complain at the quality of education of the 'school leavers' who came to them at 16. They had done school all right. They just hadn't done much education.

An inevitable trouble loomed swiftly. The 'results' (which for schools means the academic exam results) didn't get any better. In fact there were those who argued, increasingly, that they were getting worse. By 1988 the solution was clear. What we needed was an Education Reform Act, but don't let's change the education, let's change the exams! No more General Certificate of Education (GCE 'O' levels), which are elitist and disappoint those who are not allowed to enter them: no more Certificate of Secondary Education (CSE) which stigmatises those who hold it as being 'not good enough' for GCE. Instead a new examination, a comprehensive solution, the General Certificate of Secondary Education, graded of course from F, a 'pass', to A for the best. While we're at it, the girls, generally speaking, haven't been doing so well as the boys, so we'll have lots of course work and assessments over time, at which the girls are good, and fewer on the spot, in your face, now or never exams at which most of the boys are better.

Parents and employers were nearly as quick as the pupils in seeing through this one. A to C, the academic standards required for A-level, soon became the 'good pass', then became the 'pass' in their eyes and so it has remained. The academic children remained academically successful, the non-academics, especially the boys, struggled manfully to overcome the handicap of entering an academic exam based on masses of course work, some with remarkable success, the majority with the greater probability of failure. Teachers saw just as quickly that the new one size exam inevitably tended not just towards the girls, but towards the 'bottom', non-academic end, to whom it had, politically, to be made accessible in order not to be demonstrated as a fiasco. A* was the solution. All the 'bright' pupils got A* which meant that A was successfully devalued, and with it B, leaving just C as the scrape pass and everything else as an academic failure.

Still not working – we've put them into one socially acceptable school, given them socially acceptable exams, given them a year longer to do them in – it must be the teachers.

Wot, No School?

Teachers had already become perceived as no longer an elite, respected, professional force. There had been the William Tyndale scandal – in line with 1960's unstructured liberalism ('flower-power', 'all you need is love', 'peace, man') 'child centred' not teacher centred education, which seemed fine to the theorists and the teacher training colleges, but to those outside on the street to mean that teachers had abdicated their responsibilities and the children were being simply allowed to 'do their own thing', so they did pretty well nothing of what we thought they were meant to do. For extremists at the other extreme to the training colleges this meant that standards of literacy had given way to incoherent 'free expression', and standards of numeracy had given way to 'whose got the calculator?', so children wouldn't be able to read or write or spell, or add, subtract, multiply or divide.

Teachers, like most other servants of nationalised institutions of the time, had been on strike for more pay and shorter hours. Most now had little involvement with pupils in anything that went on outside the classroom and classroom hours. Low paid, little respected, all tarred with the brush of those observed annually on television shouting hysterically at Secretaries of State for Education at 'conferences', which mostly consisted of complaints and rants and unfulfilled threats to strike, they were a soft political target, easy to bash.

So we set up an inspectorate, designed to pick holes in what they did and label those schools which, inevitably, didn't deliver the 'education' we wanted them to deliver, as failing, being in need of 'special measures', responsible for the whole breakdown. That would show them.

How schools impede education

Teachers left the schools in droves, either out of the profession altogether or into independent schools where they were encouraged to teach. New teachers were harder and harder to recruit. That certainly showed them – the door.

For politicians, who were seen to be 'doing something about it', things got better, but for schools the 'results' only marginally improved: those which had children who were, or could be made to be good at school, did better; those who didn't, didn't.

So it couldn't be just the teachers it must be the curriculum as well.

Consequently, in 1988, the National Curriculum - initially entirely unworkable since we didn't trust the heads and the teachers to produce something that would work, but handed it over to the politicians and the educationalists, who produced something that wouldn't. Every teacher must teach the same thing in the same way. No room for initiative, inspired departures from the set path – not if we are to get all the boxes ticked at the right time for the inspectors - settling swiftly to the lowest common denominators, abandoning all pretence at education, seizing on a few subjects where performance (exam and test results) can easily be measured, and away with such awkward things as music, art, drama, sport, which can't, and peripherals such as Spanish or Latin at which non-academics won't be C grade successful.

Irritatingly, bored teachers and equally bored pupils didn't come up with the political goods. So a new solution. Grades must rise each year, to prove to the

Wot, No School?

voters that even if the pupils *aren't*, the government *is* doing well. Simple, make the exams easier. Maths is hard, there are fewer and fewer mathematicians who teach: even with the easier exams the pupils are still 'failing' in droves, so 'adapt' the grades. What would be a decent mark at which to wave a C grade – 33%? Way too much. 25%. Stretching it a bit. 20% Still a bit of a struggle. 15% (the 2003 academic 'pass' mark)? That should do it.

Despite all our best efforts pupils and teachers continue to let us down, even though we keep more and more of the pupils at it until they're 18 – more of the same – and now we want more and more of them to keep taking the academic medicine until they're 22…23…24… At least we no longer turn out the masses of unemployable sociologists of the 1970's. Now we turn out unemployable philosophy, psychology or media-studied 20somethings. Before long your postman, your milkman, the lorry driver and White Van Man may not be much better at delivering the goods, but at least they will all have degrees.

Recently a middle manager in a marketing organisation, himself a non-graduate, told us that whoever succeeded him in the post would need to have a degree.

We asked him why.

He couldn't say.

I could have been a chimney sweep if only I'd got the right 'A' levels.
Extract from: *In Your Dreams* Tom Holt. Reproduced by kind permission of Orbit, an imprint of Little Brown Book Group

How schools impede education

So, what will their degrees be *for*? Who can say?

School still isn't working, so we now have another raft of new initiatives, new kinds of school. There will be foundation schools, technology schools (!), specialist schools, schools which select all the pupils, schools which select some, city academies run by private enterprise, schools from which students leave from time to time to work within businesses or colleges of further education before coming back to school again, 'federation' schools which are supposed in some way to help each other out with what they can't manage on their own. We'll involve the business world, get them to pay for the new schools, in some areas we'll even pay the children to go to the schools, because they won't otherwise. And when that, as history tells us it will, goes the same way as everything else – whatever next?

Another kind of school, anyway.

All this is a well-intentioned plastering over the cracks. No one seems to be looking at the building itself. No one seems to be stopping to think that maybe it isn't the pupils, it isn't the teachers, it isn't even just the curriculum or the exams, it isn't the type of school – *it's the school itself!*

The institution, school, has become more important than the original objective, education – the drawing out of skills and capabilities.

What gets in the way of effective teaching and meaningful learning is the dehumanising institution with its panoply of academic examinations for all, regardless of interest or aptitude;

Wot, No School?

the stifling, politicised regulation of the curriculum;
the regimentation of classes and age groups;
the bureaucracy of central administration; and
the slow demoralisation of institutionalised teachers.

Teachers, hounded by bells, drowning beneath the paper
beloved of the bureaucrats,
losing the will to live in the face of each new political
'initiative', originality frowned upon, ordered to
conform, directed and inspected into '*an anodyne group:
politically correct, overworked, underfunded and not
passionate about what they do*' [William Horwood –
Author of *The Boy With No Shoes*] are close to
surrender.

Pupils learn early that there is no equality of schooling.
Pupils who come from homes where there are books,
conversation, musical instruments, a place of your own
to work, parents who support your homework, who have
all the ingredients for academic success, will succeed –
just as the Prime Minister, the Governor of the Bank of
England, the Archbishop of Canterbury, the First Sea
Lord, the Trustees of the BBC, the Secretary of State for
Children, Schools and Families (no mention of education
here!), the Minister for Standards in Schools and all the
people who decree what is success, what is failure in
school, succeeded.

For the vast majority of youngsters without those
advantages school teaches you early that you won't
succeed. For instance, more than half of children in local
authority care leave school with no GCSEs at all. In
2003 only 6% of looked-after children attained 5 or more
GCSEs and the number has not increased since then.

How schools impede education

"If at first you don't succeed – you're a failure!"
Homer Simpson

Teachers, too, know that many of their pupils are destined for school failure almost from the beginning. They may not lack intelligence, they may not lack skills and talents and aptitudes. They do lack *school* skills and they are very unlikely to acquire them. To get such pupils to pass an academic exam of any kind or of any value is going to be nearly impossible, without huge amounts of extra time, extra tuition, one-to-one help, which the teacher can't give and the parents can't afford – and all for what? To learn a lot of stuff that you'll never need to know again, so that you can satisfy some distant Whitehall paper shuffler that you can sort of do what they were good at and are, therefore, educated, employable and a credit to the system.

"...in spite of the fact that you were turned out of school at fifteen because you showed little academic skill, you may have lots of drive, good organising ability, the gift of leadership, nerves of steel and the courage of a lion. Nevertheless, because you are mystified by simultaneous equations or adverbial clauses, there is no organised route for you to take within the framework of English society. That society ordains that you are and will remain lower-class."
To England with Love by David Frost and Antony Jay, *Hodder and Stoughton. Heineman* 1967

It is hardly surprising that there has been a huge increase in the numbers of teachers, parents and pupils who are prepared to 'cheat' the system by giving pupils more and more opportunity to present course work culled by themselves (or by their parents or grandparents or siblings) from the internet, with 'model answers'

Wot, No School?

provided by teachers or downloaded from the internet exactly as they stand, left unedited and accepted as original work by teachers, even though they know it isn't. In a sentimental age in which it is demanded of teachers and parents first and foremost that they should be 'caring' can anyone be surprised that they confuse the 'caring' teacher or parent with the 'responsible' teacher or parent?

Because the school system is so rigidly founded on the notion that academic ability is of the greatest good, and that GCSE and A-level equal different degrees of intelligence, the introduction of vocational skills is instantly seen by pupils, teachers, parents and employers, as a sham, a sop for those who can't get good grades, which is what you go to school for. It isn't just that teachers are supposed to be academically good themselves. After all, if you can't get at least a C grade in GCSE in maths, (and there has been a recent call from Professor David Burghes for AS level maths for primary teachers, because this will, apparently, make them better teachers of small children, though quite how is not explained) you can't be a school teacher, however inspirational, or gifted in other areas you may be.

Teachers' training and inclination makes it hard for them to value non-academic skills and talents. If you have to do woodwork, metal work, dressmaking, commerce, or catering, even if we give them a grand title, 'vocational studies', to suggest that they are really academic subjects after all, employers believe that school has decided that you are third class, stupid, idle, good-for-nothing. Since they have got to know all about you in the 15000 hours they have had to teach you, school must be right.

How schools impede education

But it isn't.

At the moment, we have an education system which provides about 50% of students at 16 with good opportunities. These are the students who achieve 5 A*-C grades at GCSE, the standard which can determine access to further education and training courses, and jobs. The other 50% of British young people do not have these opportunities, and at a time of their lives when they should be exploring possibilities and finding open doors, they find all too many options closed to them. This is not an education system which is working well for all.

No Child Left Behind – Report of the Howson Commission into School Education August 2002

People who are good at school are often those who are good at working the system, maintaining the status quo, staying within the orthodoxies. Those who are good at school, Howson's "successful 50%", tend to go out and be good at the things that school trains them to be good at and rewards them for being good at. They become successful in the professions, as doctors, lawyers, teachers, in the Civil and other services, as accountants and adjutants, they may become councillors or MPs: they make things work smoothly, they support the system, they maintain the status quo.

But for those who were not good at school, Howson's "other 50%", whatever their intelligence, talent or aptitude, a more hazardous future beckons. At one end lie the unlucky, the criminals, the vandals, the hooligans. Above them are the erratically employed, those who make little of the restricted opportunities that school has given them and who form what Peter Morgan from the

Wot, No School?

Institute of Directors described many years ago in a speech at one of the new City Technology Colleges as the 'lumpen proletariat', which we have been 'wilfully and wastefully creating'. At the other end rise the lucky ones, who threw aside the disregard of the school system and became the movers and shakers, the founders of new businesses, the creators and the seizers of new ideas.

Scattered across the whole middle range there are engineers, artists, musicians, designers, inventors, actors, comedians, whose talents were not recognised, or were not useful at school. Some had a lucky break or two: many didn't. Some found someone, or something to motivate them to try and try, to overcome the obstacles in their path, to ignore the siren voices, 'Why bother? You can get away with doing almost nothing, with a little bit of duck and dive and dodge till something better turns up': many didn't. Some of them are successful, many are not.

Those who are successful require somewhere along the line, the lucky break. School, as we shall see in a moment, has done little to help them find or develop their skills, their aptitudes, their intelligence. It has done much to bury or blunt them.

The rules of the institution, for instance, militate against entrepreneurship.

A boy used some of his pocket money to buy a giant size bag of Maltesers in the supermarket. He also bought some shiny paper. He took the sweets out of the giant bag and wrapped them, six at a time, in twists of the shiny paper. He sold the twists to friends at school, who couldn't afford the giant bag but could

How schools impede education

afford a few pence for enough sweets for break time. When he had sold them all he put half the money into his savings and bought two more giant bags of sweets with the rest.

He was doing very well when the school found out. Whatever they may have felt about his creativity they had to stop him. They couldn't have pupils bringing money into school to tempt the bullies and the budding protection racketeers, or to create a precedent by which less scrupulous predators could prey on the innocent and unwary. It would have been acceptable for the boy to have worked out the principle in a maths or business studies lesson, but it was not acceptable for him to put theory into practice.

The rules and conditions of the institution snuffed out the ingenuity, the acumen and the hard work of its pupil. The loss to him and to us is not measurable.

At the end of an educational research visit to the United States the Head was given a lift back to the airport by one the neighbours. They travelled in a 'stretch limo' in which you had to get up and walk to the drinks cabinet. His host was a young man in his middle thirties, who, like so many people, was eager to recount his school experiences to a captive Head.

The young man had not been at all interested in whatever they taught him at school. He felt he could have acquired all that and more simply by reading it up for himself, though he did concede that he had needed someone to give him the tools with which to learn for himself. The only teacher he admired or felt beholden to was an elementary school teacher who had taught him to

Wot, No School?

read, taught him that math could be fun and taught him that, provided he completed the tasks he was set, it was good to come up with his own ideas, even if they didn't work, so long as he could explain them to someone else. For her it was the explaining that was more important, for him it was the ideas, but he had forgiven her, because she was a school teacher and explaining was what teachers did.

The other person he respected was the Head of his High School.

She was new – just like me. I walked into her office on my first day and said, "Can I do a deal with you?"

"What deal's that?"

"I won't be able to make it into school before ten in the morning. You see, I've got these two businesses, and if I don't get in first thing in the morning, they'll just sit around drinking coffee, and if there's been a problem they'll wait for me to come and tell them what to do, instead of fixing it for themselves. So, I've got to be there to get the first one started, then I've got to get across town to the other one. Then I'll come into school."

"So what's this deal, you're talking about?"

"Well, if you won't mind my not being in before ten, then I'll guarantee to get all my grades. If I don't get 'em, I'll have to come in earlier."

The new principal thought for a moment.

"OK," she said. "Only no excuses, no 'I'll get them next time'. Every grade."

How schools impede education

"Deal."

Then, at the door, departing:

"And, by the way, I'll have to leave again by 1.30"

Every grade was passed. Graduation was completed. The school work part was easy. "As long as you did what they wanted for the grade, didn't waste time figuring it out for yourself or doing anything different, it was just like being a clerk. If you put your mind to it anyone could do it in three or four hours a day. And I had to put my mind to it because I needed to get out of there and get on with the important stuff and the exciting stuff, the stuff I was good at."

In the UK, too, it seems that the system is good for developing clerks, not for developing the exciting stuff, the stuff the non-academic majority of pupils are good at. The young man in the USA had not just the good fortune to find a Head who could understand and accommodate his skills and talents, he had the good fortune to be part of a system which allowed her the freedom to do that. No state school Head in the UK would be allowed to make such an enlightened response – bevies of inspectors and school attendance officers and social workers would surround the school in an instant and bury it and its Head in mounds of papers and reports and studies for years. If young people have strong entrepreneurial or business skills in this country they are not just going to have to learn them *outside* school – they are going to have to learn them *despite* school.

It is high time that we changed that.

Chapter Four

Babies and Bathwater

Since 1944 the British education system has moved from one in which an elite was created on the basis of performance in tests at 11, with all other students academically written off, to one where one size is expected to fit all. Both of these systems are fatally flawed, and neither sufficiently addresses the needs of the "other 50%".

No Child Left Behind – Report of the Howson Commission into School Education
August 2002

Howson, whose analysis is excellent, still misses the essential point. Though the Report begins by asking, crucially, what education is for, it goes on to discuss not how to improve the education we have to offer but how to improve schools in order to improve the chances of the 'other 50%' – whose chances of a good lifetime have been, as we will show, blighted by the institution of school itself. By studying what has happened to the other 50% we can begin to see the way towards what could happen to them, the chances for a better lifetime that we could and should give them.

We have seen that, despite everything we've done to help them – despite prescribing the curriculum so that inadequate teachers can't let them down by failing to teach them the things we think they ought to be learning; despite giving them more 'pupil-friendly' exams; despite

How schools impede education

making the exams easier and easier to pass; despite giving them longer and longer at school – half of them *still* won't get it right.

So, what's the matter with them? Are they stupid or something? Why won't they learn?

'People rarely just fail to learn; they leave us with the problem of finding out what it was they were learning while they were not learning what we expected them to learn.'
Salmon and Bannister *Education for Teaching* 1974

As we look towards what we should be offering to them, to the purpose rather than the method of education, we should recognise the simplest fact that it is not that our secondary school pupils *can't* learn, it is that many of them *won't* learn what is presented to them in secondary schools. They won't do 'school' learning, but they will learn, often with unnerving speed and accuracy, not just complex computer games and skills, and everything there is to know about the Football League or the musical career of the latest bands, but also how to 'hot wire' a car, how to outwit the law, who will buy what and where to get it, how to do amazing things on a skate board etc. etc. etc.

Professor Robert Fisher, author of Teaching Thinking, tells the story of a pupil who when asked the difference between science in primary and secondary school said, "That's easy. In Year 6 we thought about it. In Year 7 we copy it off the board. When asked whether that meant he no longer liked science, he replied: "Oh no, I like *real* science. I just don't like *school* science". He had enjoyed the element of discovery and experimentation and thinking for himself in his primary class. But at secondary school, where the teachers had to ensure he 'covered the curriculum', he just copied the teachers' notes from the board and followed the prescribed orthodoxies of the science curriculum. His interest in science, in school at least, had been killed.

In a laudable desire to wash away the grime of ignorance, we have lost the infant education down the insatiable plughole of school. In order to rescue education we need to find out what 'school' is and whether it can deliver the education we believe should be available to all our children.

School isn't working

School is an institution established for the promotion of education. Though an institution's *objective* may have value, the *institution itself* has no intrinsic value. As we have seen, the institution 'school' has not only become more important than the original objective 'education', it has become confused with it. The demand is that pupils and teachers should be good at 'school', should be good inmates, good servants of the institution. Originality, thinking 'outside the box', thoughts and ideas which may change the world, creativity, innovation, things which cannot easily be measured, do not sit comfortably in such an institution. Yet, as we look towards creating an education fit for the twenty-first century, originality, creativity, innovation and discovery may be precisely what we need for the economic benefit of society and for the enrichment of our personal lives as individual human beings.

How schools impede education

The politicisation and institutionalisation of learning, and the demand that the taxpayer should pay for education, has led to the inevitable consequent demand that pupils and teachers should demonstrate that they are doing what we are paying for them to do, are giving us value for money. Since at least the excesses of the 1960's we, parents, employers, universities and increasingly panic-stricken politicians, have not been convinced that they are doing this. So, we have introduced controls and regulations to measure their performance. Inevitably, as these show that we are still not getting the results we think we want, we have introduced more and more of them, heaping measurement upon measurement in a political and bureaucratic figure-fest.

By doing this we have restricted the education we offer to young people to that which can be measured. Now teachers pursue pupils through a ritualised obstacle course towards a largely futile finishing line. Since most of the pupils are on courses entirely unsuited to their skills, talents and abilities, far too many of them don't reach the desired end at the right time, or at the right speed. Politically they must. We have to be able to say – "41.32% last year, 42.45% this year – this proves that we are a good government and you should vote for us". And if the little blighters just won't get there, we'll lower the obstacles, or give them more time. We won't change the education only the pass mark, so that many more of them will stagger across the line to universal applause. Except that they don't. And the increasingly deafening noise made by the parents, employers, universities – and the pupils themselves – doesn't sound much like applause.

Wot, No School?

Performance Indicators – The Convoy System of Education

The American professor deals with his students according to his lights. It is his business to chase them along over a prescribed ground at a prescribed pace like a flock of sheep. They all go humping together over the hurdles with the professor chasing them with a set of 'tests' and 'recitations', 'marks' and 'attendances', the whole apparatus obviously copied from the time-clock of the business man's factory. This process is what is called 'showing results'. The pace set is necessarily that of the slowest, and thus results in what I have heard Mr Edward Beatty describe as the 'convoy system' of education.

Stephen Leacock from *My Discovery of England (1922)*

In order to become a successful institution a school has to be able to publish successful 'performance indicators'. These indicators are set by a central organisation outside the school.

The school itself is not part of the goal-setting procedure, the goals and targets are not theirs, they are not even suited to the talents and abilities of the pupils within them – governments and their civil servants set the goals and the targets for the institution and then send their inspectors to inspect its success, or lack of it, in reaching the goals. No one can be surprised at the lack of success, the number of schools that have to go into 'special measures' in order to get them to achieve the government's targets and goals.

For instance, 'League tables' for schools measure the number of Year 11 pupils who achieve 5 of the academic

How schools impede education

A*-C grades, clearly the grades that matter to the government. They don't measure the performance of individual pupils, just the performance of the school. Year after year 50% (plus or minus 2 or 3 per cent) achieve this government goal. 50% don't.

Now, the 'performance indicators' do not just measure the education provided, they determine what is taught in schools. Now, what our children have to learn there, the 'education' which must be provided for them, consists only of that which can be measured.

> *... our education is falling foul of what has been called the McNamara fallacy, after the US Secretary of Defense in the Vietnam War, who said that what gets counted is what counts but, more importantly, that what doesn't get counted or can't easily be counted is ignored. This, he said, is suicide. Any good manager knows better that to rely only on numerical targets as a measure of performance is dangerous for that very reason. I believe that our education is seriously distorted by the passion for exam results and league tables.*
> [Professor Charles Handy – *Personal communication*]

The latest twist to this measurement fest is that schools are to be judged on whether 30% of their pupils get five GCSE passes at grades A* - C. If they fail, they face the threat of closure irrespective of where they are located and what kind of pupil intake they have. The result is that an awful lot of time is being spent on those young people whose forecast results are in the grade C to D range – no doubt at the expense of those with higher expectations or of those with no hope.

At the younger age range Standard Assessment Tests (SATs) achieve a similar government triumph, or a similar school failure. Originally, no individual pupil's results were published, except to parents who ask for them, only those of the institution.

When the government of the day introduced the National Curriculum, independent schools were specifically excluded from the requirements of the Education Reform Act. They had to 'opt in' if they wanted to join the government's new, streamlined, reformed educational system.

At each of the various meetings with government representatives to explain the glories of the new system an independent school Head asked the same two questions. One was about the National Curriculum itself: "What good reasons can you give me to take back to my teachers, my parents, my governors and my pupils to convince them that we should opt in?"

None of them could say.

The other was about the system of measurement. "Can you tell me what value it is to a future employer, or a place of further or higher education, to know about a student with GCSE or 'A' levels what that student was doing at age 7, or 11?"

"We shan't publish pupils' individual results, so they won't know, anyway."

"So, why are the pupils taking them?"

"So that we can measure the schools' performance."

The institution was openly declared as of more significance than the people within it, the 'results' more important to the government than the education to the

How schools impede education

pupils – never mind the education, look at the percentages… No one outside the school would be interested in how Jack or Jill is doing in their SATs. All anyone would want to know would be, how many pupils in the school are achieving at, or above or below the government's prescribed level in the government's tests? How Jill is doing, how Jack is doing, what Jill is doing, what Jack is doing was immaterial. How the institution is doing was what mattered.

Since then, of course, SATs results *have* been published and the ludicrous inadequacies of the tests (and the marking system!) were revealed to all, with the result that SATs at age fourteen have now been summarily cancelled and there is a good chance that they will be dropped for 11 year olds soon and England will be brought into line with the much more sensible Welsh and Scots.

The National Curriculum, designed to ameliorate the effects of what were perceived to be the worst teachers, has resulted in the loss of freedom for good teachers to teach and to inspire, and, in another shining example of the Law of Unintended Consequences, the increasing loss of many of the best teachers.

Professor Ted Wragg, emeritus professor of education at Exeter University, said: *"People's confidence has been shot to pieces. This is what happens when you browbeat a profession for a long time. The high stakes of league tables and inspections have created a cowed profession when people for formal purposes, follow everything to the letter, terrified of putting a foot wrong. It is like Brave New World where the people become*

Wot, No School?

defenders of the system that oppressed them. It is a 21st –century tragedy. The profession has to stand up and say to politicians to go and boil their collective heads."
Times Educational Supplement July 23 2004

As with the secondary school exam measurement system teachers in 'SATS years' know that they have to spend a disproportionate amount of the time available to them 'teaching the exam' rather than teaching the children. Teachers don't want to *instruct* – especially what pupils not only don't want to learn but know won't be of any use to them once they have escaped the institution – but, if they are going to be *school* teachers, they have to. Their working lives depend on it.

Thousands of the teachers have fled, most reluctantly. The pupils have had to remain behind.

*"Education in this country will never function effectively until pupils, **at least at secondary level, can choose their areas of study** and do not spend every day wastefully being forced to learn much of what they do not want to know."*
A J Marsden, Bury, Lancs.
Extract from letter to the Times Educational Supplement
[Our emphasis]

This is what we must aim to change; to free our teachers to teach and our children to learn what is of value to *them*, not to the men with the measuring sticks.

Far too many children experience the debilitating, de-motivating frustration of receiving little or no education in the things that will matter to them in living fulfilled adult lives. So we have to decide what things do matter.

How schools impede education

One parent wants her daughter to score highly in the SATs; another wants energetic, inspirational teaching. Yet schools are increasingly aware that these two aims are not compatible. Teachers busy aiming for targets and test results become drained of their will to inspire and enthuse.... Could it be that the styles of teaching being used in pursuit of educational targets simply don't suit a significant proportion of children? I don't know that we have found a way to have very tight measurements and maintain creativity...

Tracey Ruddle, Primary School Head, writing in T2
August 11 2004

Far too many children have little time to:
explore with their teachers music, art, drama, sport (how much of the newspapers, the television, the media in the adult world is taken up with these activities? how much at school?);
try out something new, follow their interests, grow from different ideas;
learn how to think;
learn the things that their teachers would love to teach them, at the rate which would be most challenging for them, to the limits of their current capability;
find out what their skills and talents and aptitudes are;
taste success in areas which are not academic, not 'school' skills - rather than learn that they are not good at 'school' and that, therefore, they are not going to be good at life.

"Examinations are a tremendous obstacle to education taking place. They force every child to be one kind of child, and the school to create a system which subordinates real education to an artificial exercise called 'passing exams'. Children are as different as flowers in a garden. Some flowers are tall, some broad,

Wot, No School?

some bright coloured, some fragrant, some hardy, some luxuriant; some children are quick-minded, some clever with their hands, some creative, some good at games, some natural leaders; all are also a combination of some of the other qualities. Real education helps each child to develop and use his own qualities as fully as possible, just as good horticulture treats each plant with lime or peat or bone meal, much or little water, sun or shade, thinning or pruning, to help it to its best state. The skill of education and horticulture lies in different treatments. But exams are about similarity, arbitrarily picking one or two characteristics and attaching all the importance to them, so that (educationally) carnations may go through their whole lives with a stigma of inferiority because they weren't hollyhocks."

To England with Love *Ibid.*

If our concern is truly with education, rather than with indicators, we have to enable the ones who aren't good at academic subjects, aren't good at school maths, or school science, or school English, but who are good at sport, or creative or performance arts, who can perform mental practical calculations at high speed, or who have an enviable manual dexterity or ability to make things work, or to get other people to work for them, to escape the labels we give them, 'slow', 'under-achieving' or, in the parlance of the playground, 'thick', and to grow in achievement, success and personal fulfilment.

There must also be no question of the gifted pupil, gifted in whatever field, *'hanging back till the last sheep has jumped over the fence. He need wait for no one. He may move forward as fast as he likes, following the bent of his genius'* [Stephen Leacock Ibid.]

How schools impede education

If primary education requires a reconstruction of the school in which it is to take place, to release the priceless gift of the teachers to teach and the children to learn, then the bell has tolled for secondary schools.

In recent years the curriculum has become ever more prescriptive as successive governments have sought to prove their own success through the success of students in exams. Whilst we would never want to return to a system where over half of 11 year-olds are deemed failures because of their performance in one set of tests, we do recognise that people's interests and abilities are too complex to be addressed in one rigid system. Therefore we want to create a system where all students have appropriate choices about which routes to follow, and where they are supported and encouraged in following the path which is most suited to them.
No Child Left Behind – Report of the Howson Commission

Losing Our Heads

Heads, too, know that they are in an essentially 'no-win' situation. If their pupils do well, people complain that the exams are too easy. If their pupils do badly, parents complain that it is the school's fault. If they do a magnificent job in simply getting most of their pupils to come into school most of the time and, if they give all those pupils a chance to have a crack at the exams (however inappropriate and 'unwinnable' the exams are to however many of them), the inspectors will put them into 'special measures' because they haven't got enough of them to get 'enough' academic passes.

Wot, No School?

A former Head Teacher visited the Head of a large secondary school, situated on the edge of a sprawling, 'difficult' estate. The retired Head was impressed by the determination of the school to offer experiences to the students in the arts, in sports, in cultural and social experiences in non-academic areas. He admired their significant success in bringing in so many reluctant attendees so often, from an estate which delivered all the messages of hopelessness and apathy and living 'off the benefit' until you were old enough to profit from the proceeds of crime. There were trees and grass and uniforms, mostly decent order and a ceaseless struggle to raise sufficient self esteem among young people for whom the GCSE battle would be largely unwinnable, and for whom A-levels could occasionally be glimpsed on the passing backs of flying pigs, to have a go at the exams anyway.

The former Head's business could not be completed because of an imminent inspection, but he arranged to come again when the dust had settled. The next term he telephoned. The Head was unable to make an appointment. He was besieged by inspectors, support teams and consultants. His school had failed its inspection on the grounds of the high proportion of students who had not achieved the government required GCSE 'passes'. They were in 'special measures' and sinking fast. Teachers were seeking posts elsewhere. The Head himself would be on his way as soon as he could.

Some years later, despite all the expertise, support and extra funding the school still bumps along at the bottom of the league tables.

But if Heads, in the interests of a good league table position, decide not to try to get the pupils in, and to hide

How schools impede education

them from the inspectors and GCSEs…

The inspection team were in a spot of bother. Their car had broken down, they were due at the school in half an hour and they were still some three or four miles away in distinctly hostile territory. They wound up the windows and ensured the doors were locked. The driver called the breakdown company. It was rush hour. They would have to wait. The car was becoming steamed up. Someone wound a window down a little.

A youth of about 14 had been slumped on some railings watching them. He sauntered over. They prepared to wind the window up again. "Broken down, mate?" he enquired, affably. Slightly less apprehensive they admitted they were.

"What's wrong?"

The driver, who knew about as much about cars as a politician knows about education, gave a vague summary of what had happened, "…and then it just stopped."

"Open it up," the youth said, slouching round to the front of the car. He paused and came back. "It's the red handle," he said, "Under the steering wheel."

"Oh, yes, of course. How stupid of me…"

"Yeah," he said. Odd noises clunked under the raised bonnet. A spotty face came round the side. "Give it a go," it said. The engine spluttered, hesitated, jerked into life.

"Can we give you something?"

"Nah, 's all right, mate."

Wot, No School?

"We must have made you late for school. Can we give you a lift in?"

"Nah, don't bother mate, me and my mates aren't going in today."

"Why's that?"

"Been told not to. They've got the inspectors in so they've told us to keep out this week."

When they put the school into special measures, the inspectors cited attendance rates as one of the main failings.

Under the circumstances, who, in his right mind, would be a Head?

"Head Teacher turnover is reaching critical proportions... There are not the candidates queuing up to replace them... The government knows it has a crisis on its hands. But has yet to come up with an answer..."
David Hart, General Secretary NAHT April 2004

A survey taken by the National Association of Head Teachers in the school year 2005/6 showed that more than 1200 state schools were without a full-time head.

Maybe the Heads and the Deputy Heads and the teachers will do it for us.

Maybe they will succeed in abolishing the secondary school, with its inbuilt inability to educate at least 50% of our children satisfactorily, entirely – as well as the primary school in its current form. So, maybe we had better have something better in its place before we lose not only the schools, but the teachers.

We can lose *schools* happily but if we lose *teachers* we lose *education* itself.

*

A Royal Society for the encouragement of Arts, Manufactures & Commerce (RSA) report entitled Education for Capability (1985) concluded that: *"A well-balanced education should, of course, embrace analysis and acquisition of knowledge. But it must also include the exercise of creative skills, the competence to undertake and complete tasks and the ability to cope with everyday life; and also doing these things in co-operation with others."*

There was no indication at the time that anyone disagreed with this analysis, yet twenty years later, hamstrung by the secondary school and the academic exam system, though we still 'embrace analysis and acquisition of knowledge' (however valuable that knowledge or those analytical skills may be for everyone who has to embrace them) we still have done almost nothing about the rest, though the RSA itself is now taking a lead with its 'competence-led curriculum'.

Chapter Five

Schools or Education?

So, how do government and the media measure schools?
A case in point might be the increasing furore over the
introduction and funding of one of the latest wheezes,
the City Academies. Despite the millions of pounds of
private and public money being poured into them they
are, according to their opponents, clearly not cost-
effective. They may, say their supporters, have begun
slowly but they are clearly improving the lot of the
pupils within them. How do they measure this cost-
effectiveness, these improvements? Not by the education
they provide, but by the increase or otherwise in the
number of GCSE's, particularly at the academic pass
grades A*-C, achieved by the pupils.

Their very title 'Academies' tell us that they are not
there to educate pupils but to find ways of getting more
of them through more academic examinations, regardless
of whether they are naturally academic or not, regardless
of whether academic learning, an academic teaching
style, or academic testing is beneficial to them or to us or
to anybody except the officials with the measuring
sticks.

Government officials, the media or the pundits wheeled
out to raise their hands in horror at the poor GCSE
results tell us nothing about the teachers' success or

otherwise in opening up the multifarious skills and talents of the pupils; about the enrichment of the young people's educational experiences; about the number of books they have read (not for examination purposes but for enjoyment or interest); the number and quality of any artefacts they may have produced (not for the Art or Design exams but for enjoyment or interest or out of curiosity or to solve a problem or improve a game, or a show, or to make something work better); the number and quality of the exhibitions, the plays, the shows, the concerts, the 'gigs', the individual and group productions they have performed in, or for which they have provided the props, the lighting, the costumes or the effects; the number, quality and popularity of the 'clubs' and 'activities' that they run, the films the pupils have seen, or the films they have made, or the galleries they have visited, or the range and quality of their participation in sports; the number and quality of new ideas generated among pupils and teachers; the number, range and quality of their inventions and innovations and working models and whether they were successful or not; the differences that young people and teachers have made to the environment, or to the society, or to the families in which they live and move and have their being.

Where are we to discover the number of pupils who learn to play musical instruments, or compose songs or tunes (but not for an examination); or who draw, or paint or design clothes or buildings or boats or cars or games; or who learn DIY skills or solve (or try to solve) practical problems posed by local services, organisations, businesses? Where do we find records of the quality of their debates, or the questions they asked of local councillors or MPs, or the charitable work they have done? How do we know about the number of kids who participate in a dozen activities, the number who participate in next to nothing and what the Academy does about that? Where do we find out about what the pupils tried, what they succeeded in, what defeated them and how they responded to that; about the talents they discovered, maybe unexpectedly, that they possessed, about the talents they knew they had and developed, about the things that they did that excited them, or astonished themselves as well as the adults around them?

If you want to know the percentage increase or decrease in GCSE or A-level results you will readily be provided with a number of statistics and a variety of 'spins' to interpret those statistics. If you want to know about anything else you will have to work hard to find it.

The implication is that none of these things we have mentioned, nor any of the other things you and we might consider valuable as part of an educational experience, form any significant part of the school's business, or are worth mentioning alongside their GCSE results: none of these activities or learning opportunities is central to their education, merely peripheral activities around the real business of proving that pupils are or are not able to tackle academic examinations in a way that is acceptable to the Department for Education and Skills and that therefore that they are, or are not succeeding at the things worth succeeding at.

This is not a view that has gone altogether unchallenged even by government officials themselves. In 1943 they wrote in a publication called *Educational Reconstruction*:

How schools impede education

Instead of the schools performing their proper and highly important function of fostering the potentialities of children at an age when their minds are nimble and perceptive, their curiosity strong, their imagination fertile and their spirits high, the curriculum is too often cramped and distorted by over-emphasis on examination subjects and on ways and means of defeating the examiners. **The blame for this rests not with the teachers but with the system.** [Our emphasis.]

This underlines that for more than forty years at least, the further implication has been that 'school' is for passing academic or 'vocational' exams and tests and qualifications to enable pupils to 'go to Uni' (to spend longer doing more of the same) or to 'get a good job' (to start earning money sooner). Given the perennial blurring of the 'school' and 'education' notions, the implication is that that is what education is for, too.

If we are content with that view, if we are content that that is what we mean by and want from schools, if we are content that that is what we mean by and want from education, then we will have to learn to be content with Howson's 'other fifty per cent' who, like the poor, will always be with us. We will have to be content with leaving the emergence of the majority of most people's talents to chance. We will continue to create a more or less permanent 'under class' (Jay and Frost's 'lower class') of the thousands of children who leave school with no discernible qualifications at all – let alone any academic ones – and little chance of a fulfilled lifetime. We will have to accept the inevitable inequality of schooling that will keep delivering us what it has delivered us and what we have complained about for the last century or more. The schooling 'have's' will continue to have – only more so – the 'have nots' will just have to put up with the endlessly demonstrated fact that they are no good at school and destined to be no good at life since it seems that they are going to be offered no other form of education.

On the other hand...

We might pause, before plunging in to the creation of yet another type of school, to consider what we might want education, as opposed to school to be for.

Society and school

It is part of the history of human progress that human beings have always tended to want to push forward, to explore new places, new ideas, new possibilities. Sometimes these advances and expansions were compelled by circumstances. Necessity has frequently been the mother of movement and expansion as well as invention. Local resources may be insufficient to sustain a growing population so we move out to find new lands. We dig in the earth to find new resources, we explore the seas for food and minerals and fuels, we take a few tentative steps towards the edges of the universe.

Over the last few decades as the possibilities for external exploration have shrunk, or have become too costly, we have begun to explore inwards into the greatest human resource, the human brain. This is not the place for a detailed study of the research that has been done and the discoveries that have been made but let us merely note that over the last half dozen decades more research has been done into the way the human brain works, how human beings think and create and the nature of human intelligence than in all of previous human history. How far has our schooling and examination process taken note and developed from this research and new understanding of what might constitute human intelligence and brain power?

Similarly for adults living in the western world, the world of the technologically advanced nations, the nature of the lives they lead and the work they do has changed over a similar period of time at a greater rate than ever before. In the very broadest terms, the old agricultural economy which held sway for millennia has been replaced in the last two or three centuries first by the industrial, mass manufacturing economy and then in the last few decades by the technological and service economy, the economy of knowledge, invention, discovery and innovation. How far has our schooling and examination process taken note and developed from this enormous change in the requirements that will be needed for the possible careers and the future social lives their pupils might have the opportunity to lead?

Part of the problem may be that the schooling we receive in our formative years as children and especially as adolescents, as we have reiterated, focuses on a limited area of human intelligence, the academic, reasoning powers, the logical-mathematical and the linguistic intelligences which we engage, test and examine through our panoply of academic examinations at 11, 16, 18, 22 and so on. It does little to find, develop, or educate those other intelligences which are so much harder to measure, but are to do with the constructive, the exploratory, the creative, the aesthetic, the moral, the social, and the spiritual elements of a human life. It is far too easy for us to write-off a significant proportion of our school pupils, to label them as 'failures' because they are not good at the type of education we offer them and, therefore they are not 'bright'.

But do not let our natural inclination to pair opposites lead us to conclude that if they are not academically 'bright' they must therefore be 'stupid' or 'thick'. Even given the fact that such words are politically incorrect and thus dare not be spoken openly, that does not make them the right words. We all know many examples of almost incandescently bright people who were hopeless at school.

"...incandescently bright people who were hopeless at school."

Vivian Hill - Director of Professional Educational Psychology, Institute of Education, University of London - at the end of the last programme of *The*

How schools impede education

Unteachables (a television documentary series, led by the late and much lamented Professor Ted Wragg, about a group of those children already written off by themselves as well as by their schools and in many cases by their families) during which she was the resident Educational Psychologist helping the kids - and teachers - get through it all, said:

"Our education system is very much based on an academic model of learning and middle class principles, and these don't necessarily apply to everybody in the system. What we are needing to do now is to recognise different styles of learning and education and introduce different types of educational experience; I know some people might find that horrendous, and worry that we might have an apartheid education system, but clearly this one-size-fits-all isn't working for quite a lot of our young people."

Though, in our proposal, there is no need for an 'apartheid education system', simply an education system that is fit for everyone's purpose, how right she was, and is!

It is salutary for us to recall the enormous, untapped potential that resides in the brains of these apparent 'failures'. Colin Rose, in his fascinating book 'Accelerated Learning' (published in 1985 by Accelerated Learning Systems Ltd., Aylesbury, Bucks, updated and reprinted many times since then) which is mainly about the role of memory in learning and with ways in which to improve its depth and efficiency, describes this potential very simply and effectively:

… the proportion of our potential brain power that we use is probably nearer 4% than 10%. Most of us…

Wot, No School?

appear to let 96% of our mental potential lie unused…
But it doesn't have to be so… The average adult human
brain consists of some 12,000 million to 15,000 million
nerve cells [neurons]. … The power of the brain is
largely a function of the <u>number</u> of neurons and the
<u>richness</u> of their connections. Since each neuron can
itself make thousands of connections, the potential
number of interconnections in the brain runs into
trillions. The key point to remember is that only some of
these connections are made automatically. Most are
made by using the brain. The more your brain is
stimulated, the richer the connections and the higher
your practical mental ability…

Later, he writes that there is conclusive evidence that:
'…the provision of constant stimuli improves mental
ability'.

It is necessary to be *involved* in mental exercise, to
experiment directly with new ideas.

So, if we could stimulate the brains of the 'failures', the
'no-hopers', the 'dumbos' of our schooling system, the
ones with a mere 12 billion neurons; if we could involve
them in a wide range of mental activities in which they
could become active participants with a realistic chance
of winning, rather than spectators of the 'bright' kids
ability to cope with the approved subject matter and the
approved style of learning; if we could improve the
richness of their educational environment and the
richness of the interconnections between their brain cells
by as little as one per cent, then their practical mental
ability, their 'brain power' might expand to the levels of
those we currently hold to be the brightest and the best.
And if we could all seek for ways to tap into at least a
little of that 'idling' 96% for everyone…

How schools impede education

At school in the early and middle parts of the twentieth century students might have done well at woodwork and cooking, but may not do so well in the modern school in Design or Food Technology (vocational studies which sound academic enough to be allowed to take place in a school, rather than vocational skills which don't), where you have to know what to do and sometimes why it should be done the approved way, rather than know how, or be able actually to do it.

While we should remember that almost everyone has the *potential* to acquire skills and capabilities in many different areas, it is clear that those who have the aptitude or who are fortunate enough to have the extrinsic motivators (a stable home with books, music, a place to work, encouragement from and regular conversation with their parents) to develop particular strengths in the areas that are useful for triumph in the government's limited idea of education are the ones who will do well at 'school'. The rest will just have to struggle to achieve a half decent set of exam results if they want the acclamation of teachers, parents and politicians and the offers of university places.

It is equally necessary for us to remember that, though the academic 'school' system is geared especially to the two left brain, linguistic, logical-mathematical parts of the brain, *all* parts can and do contribute to the *thinking* process. Otherwise we would be in danger of falling into the trap which almost ruined a US company which applied 'intelligence' tests to all its employees in order to weed out the least able and found out only just in time that they were about to sack all the artists in the design office!

Wot, No School?

It is no accident that our material success is largely due to the fact that we are trained to think in a pattern we call logical, and… this seems to mainly involve one side of the brain – the left side. Conversely our learning methods are not designed to stimulate the development of the side of the brain that processes concepts – the right side. So our success in logical, material pursuits is perhaps not surprising – nor is our comparative failure in conceptual ethical issues. [Accelerated Learning – *Colin Rose*]

The authors of this book know from our own experience what happens when we ask a group of school teachers to identify the most able pupils in their school, choosing from these categories: Physical talent; Mechanical ingenuity; Visual abilities; Performing abilities; Outstanding leadership skills; Social awareness; Creativity; and High intelligence. Teachers have no difficulty in identifying high intelligence – in their own subject areas anyway. However, secondary school teachers in particular frequently struggle with at least some of the other categories, especially with mechanical ingenuity, visual abilities and, for those who do not teach in the 'Arts subjects' or sports areas, with creativity. Given the nature of their jobs and their duties, this is hardly surprising. Unless it is of demonstrable value to them to know of these other abilities it merely serves as a distraction from their requirement to get as many of their pupils as possible through as high grades as possible in forthcoming public examinations, about which they are extremely caring and conscientious.

It is no more surprising that in most schools right brain dominant activities, like art and music and drama, gradually lose their place in the curriculum offered to all pupils from a good base in the earliest years of primary schooling until they are down (if they are lucky) to maybe an hour of art, and half an hour of music and drama per week in the years before GCSE work begins. Many have less than that. Yet secondary schools which have dared, in defiance of the prescripts of the government's National Curriculum, to increase the proportion of 'arts' subjects and lessons find that levels of performance improve right across the subject range. As we have already noted, independent schools, most of which tend to cling on to sports and arts provision for far longer and in far greater depth, frequently seem to achieve better 'results' for average or 'lower ability' pupils than might be the case with their equivalents in state maintained schools which do not have the freedom to manipulate their curricula in this way. Though state school teachers are well aware of the research and its implications for a fulfilling education for their pupils, their institutions are under immense league-table pressure to secure 'good academic results' in public examinations, or face remedial action or worse, from the equally government-bound inspectorate, and mostly find it very hard to take full advantage of the possibilities for teachers and pupils.

Information and Knowledge

In a modern education it should be more important to learn how to interpret information rather than to accumulate information; to think about facts rather than merely to know facts, to develop soundly based opinions rather than to be able to repeat the 'right' answers. What we need is the ability to think, rather than just to receive or to regurgitate. We can probably all remember the teacher or parent who railed at us 'Think, boy!' or 'You

Wot, No School?

just don't think, child', but we may not find it so easy to remember which teachers, if any, taught us how to do it. Nonetheless it is arguable that the increasingly mechanistic academic GCSE and A-levels, intent upon getting more pupils to achieve better grades, have little to do with thinking and that teachers can still acquire the best results for their institutions by spoon-feeding pupils through teacher-regulated learning to improve their grades. However, universities still tend to want their students to think and more and more of them openly admit that, for other than the most highflying academically elite universities for which almost all candidates require at least an A grade in almost every subject, A-level results are not such good indicators of degree success as are the ability to think through new knowledge and the mental qualities of persistence, perseverance, self-organisation, and a focused clarity of aim and ambition.

The areas of 'imaginative', creative and divergent thinking may be the ones we most need to cultivate if we are to live happy and fulfilled lives as adults. They may also be the least well served by insistence upon an academic style of learning and teaching for everyone. *'Divergent thinking'* wrote J. P. Guildford in *"Traits of Creativity"* [in Creativity and Its Cultivation edited by H. H. Anderson, Harper, New York 1959] *'...is characterised... as being less goal-bound. There is freedom to go off in different directions... Rejecting the old solution and striking out in some direction is necessary, and the resourceful organism will more probably succeed'*. In the School Leaving Certificate and Personal Education system, which we outline in the subsequent chapters of this book, there are many chances for teachers and learners to strike out in new directions,

How schools impede education

uninhibited by the need to reduce almost everything to the requirements of essentially convergent thinking examinations (where there is almost always one 'right' answer or conclusion to which the thinking must lead) which are the overriding measures of success.

Schools for whom the percentage of A* to C, or the A-level A and B grades are vital, often to their very survival, have little incentive, sometimes a positive disincentive to explore thinking, especially imaginative, creative and divergent thinking, in all its range, depth, variety and subtlety, with pupils whom they have to force through the government's approved examinations. It is hard for a GCSE or A-level style examination to offer candidates the opportunity successfully to demonstrate imagination, creativity, originality or divergent ideas beyond the approved orthodoxies.

In the face of all this change, schools themselves have hardly changed at all. A Victorian child transported into a modern school might marvel at the technology, at the comfort of the furnishings and the lighting and the heating, at the physical size and health of the pupils and their freedom to disrupt the teachers. But they would immediately recognise the place as a school, with teachers and pupils and bells and lessons and play times all at the same time as one another and terms and starting ages and leaving ages and registers, things to be learned from texts and repeated as accurately as possible in order to pass exams and go on to the next school, or not, according to your ability to carry out a narrow range of activities to the levels approved by the teachers before you (and the school inspectors behind them!). The content may have changed according to the knowledge available to the teachers and to society: the requirements

Wot, No School?

for examination success may have become harder, or may have been 'dumbed down' to suit the times and the contemporary expectations of teachers and society, but the general approach, the general activities have barely changed at all. And yet the working and social lives the Victorian children and the 21st century children go on to lead are enormously different in content, style, pace, scope and range of opportunities.

It might be useful to note some of the views expressed in a four part series published in early 2005 by *The Times Educational Supplement* asking the question 'What is education for?' Most of the articles in this series seemed to be about either what was happening in schools, or about structures and different types of schooling, tinkerings with the system, or pleas for more study in the areas of the specialism or of particular interest to the writers, or suggesting ways in which schools might change in the future. Comparatively few of them addressed the question of education *per se* and what we want from it.

Tony Benn, asked the question, answered it succinctly and thoughtfully as ever:
"*1. To discover and realise the genius in everyone. 2. To learn about the people in the world with whom you have to live and their history and culture. 3. To acquire the skills to do the work you want. 4. To build up your confidence in yourself. 5. To discover the danger of hate and the power of love.*"

Though we would agree with him that taken together these answers might provide an argument for comprehensive education we are not so sure as he seems

How schools impede education

to be that they have been well served by comprehensive schools, or, perhaps by most schools, for most children. Professor Helen Storey, an artist and ex fashion designer, said:

"Education has a responsibility not to let a single child leave school without a clear idea of where their gift or skill lies and some tangible experience and a defined forward path of how to develop it... The truant who is more interested in outside life may be a frustrated entrepreneur, and the child who flourishes at home but not in school may be gifted in ways the current curriculum cannot cater for..."

Sir Digby Jones, Director General CBI, perhaps spoke for many business people and parents when he wrote:

"Education is to prepare you for life... It is certainly there to give a set of basic values – honesty, peace, selflessness... [it] should teach young people how to understand risk. If it fails to do that then there will be a nasty shock when they come into the world... [it] has to equip people for a competitive world..."

How many of these ideals are served by our current insistence that everyone should pursue an academic education into further education and almost everyone should go on to a university education thereafter?

In our confusion over the role of schools we have begun to add more and more to our requirements of them. We haven't altered or adapted their core activities, considered the desirability of the education they provide – we have simply added extra, sometimes seemingly conflicting duties for them to perform. Claire Fox, Director of the Institute of Ideas when asked the question, 'What is education for?' responded with her concerns about what is happening to schooling:

Wot, No School?

"...The ideal of a cultural transmission of knowledge has been sidelined by a new set of aims, such as tackling obesity, creating active citizens, and combating social exclusion and low self esteem. As schools become littered with behaviour improvement consultants, anti-bullying counsellors and healthy eating instructors, it feels as though schools have become a new vehicle for an official behaviour modification scheme."

The emergence of a new idea, the 'extended' or 'full-service school', open Monday to Friday from 6.30 am to 8.30pm, as well as on Saturdays, and offering nursery and childcare facilities, as well as a place for older students to do homework or receive study support, and opportunities for adult learning, with links to FE colleges, health workers, police and social services, seem to support her argument. She may well be right to be concerned by the conflicts of aims and targets of all these different government agencies competing for space, time and funding, leaving no one sure who is in charge of what, that such things might not just have all the makings of a bureaucratic heaven or hell but might not be the province of *schools* as organisations set up to impart knowledge and skill to children. However, should it not be the concern of *education* to reduce the possibilities of social exclusion, to give young people a proper estimation of their own value and of the range of their skills, talents and aptitudes, to enable them to choose and modify their own behaviour to other people, or give them a better chance of understanding themselves and the effects of the life styles they might or might not choose?

Not many of the articles considered the question of the weight schools should give to the role of creativity, the spiritual, moral, social and cultural aspects of education

How schools impede education

– the 'why is this? wherefor? what should we do?' which can give greater meaning to adult life. It is, however, pertinent to what follows, that those who showed the most concern for these aspects were those who taught in primary education, before the dead hand of public-academic-examinations-for-all falls upon all our children as they enter the secondary system. For example, this is Anna House, a Primary School Head teacher on the subject of the purposes of education:

"It's about learning how to learn, asking searching questions and seeking answers; finding out about the world, sharing your knowledge, understanding and ideas with others, both at home and in school; learning, practising and refining skills in an environment of high expectations…

"[It] should help you form values, to develop empathy and tolerance, encourage passions and enthusiasms, experience the joy of making music with others, create works of art, dance and drama, the fun of playing in a team, designing and making, being a philosopher, photographer or film-maker, a naturalist or gardener. It's about becoming inspired by the power of the written and the spoken word, solving mathematical problems or marvelling at an insect under a microscope.

"Much of what is essential to nourish young hearts and minds has been neglected…."

We felt a strong affinity for the views of Professor James Tooley, Professor of Education at Newcastle University:

"Education is for human flourishing… to flourish as a human being, you will probably want to be initiated into the best that has been thought and said – the traditions of knowledge… Second, to flourish you will benefit from the instrumental, personal and social roles that education can bring; personal empowerment, becoming equipped for the adult world of family life, work, politics, and personal and social responsibilities.

Wot, No School?

Education in both these respects has been corrupted by two tyrannies: that of schooling and that of the state. Schooling is part of the institutional mechanisms which the state has either created or set in stone, for purposes which may or may not relate to education... So when governments tell us what we need from education [read schooling], we should resist their clarion calls. **What we need from education is to take part in the conversation between the generations and to become empowered as social beings and as individuals.**" [Our emphasis.]

Universities and the Academics

So far we have concentrated more on that majority of young people who are let down by that element of the present, inequitable system, which insists that academic ability is of the greatest good – but only while you are incarcerated in school. Giving proper opportunities to the wastefully lost intelligences and aptitudes of the current have-nots should be the first concern of everyone truly interested in education for all people. Sadly, more people involved in the administration or politics of education seem more interested in tinkering with academic examinations or in refining the chances of the academic 'haves' than in getting to grips with all the other forms of intelligence, or in releasing the equally exciting powers of the creative, practical, 'know how', movers and shakers.

However, it would be just as wasteful not to seek further to enhance the prospects of the academic minority who will, we hope, go on to explore, define and discover truths about science and society, our past and our future, to give meaning to the works by which we are known. It

How schools impede education

is, perhaps, inevitable that, in the anxiety to lift the 'academic examination' chances of the naturally non-academic, our educationalists have been concentrating on the bottom end of the academic spectrum, thereby restraining the freedoms of the top end, high flying thinkers, the future researchers and pushers-back of the boundaries of knowledge, the explorers of the mind and the heart, in the name of a false equality, drawing everyone into the same homogenous sludge. Increasingly mechanistic academic public examinations encourage 'spoon-feeding', teacher regulated learning rather than the self-regulated learning, the precision and rigour, the scepticism and the divergent thinking required of our best analytic, abstract thinkers and researchers, our genuine academics.

Employment by Degrees

The insistence on an education at least academic in name for all has seen a steady increase in the number, if not the sharpness of the pinnacles of academe, the universities. Parents, students and tax payers have also seen the escalating cost to young people and their families of a place at 'uni' become of no clearly definable value to large numbers of the non-academically inclined, as successive governments have sought to pump up the figures of those who stay on into further and higher education - to what end? To bolster our place in the European or World league tables? To provide more people with largely useless 'degrees'? To massage the unemployment figures?

Once we have put in place the opportunities provided by the 'ladder' system which leads up to the School Leaving Certificate, and by the freedoms to go further

Wot, No School?

offered by Personal Education, we need no longer be shackled to the notion that the more young people we can force into a university education the better and brighter they will all become, so that eventually everyone must go to a university in order to get a proper education. The outcome, as we are already seeing, is more and more young people and parents haunted by the spectre of debt, more and more complaints about inferior university courses, inferior university teaching, more and more 'dumbing down' to ensure that fewer and fewer 'drop out' having wasted some of the best years of their lives drifting through a largely unwanted and often largely pointless course with no apparent advantage gained at the end of it. In employment terms an increasing number of young people are already finding out that by going to the inevitable 'uni' course they are losing out to those who had a clear idea of what they wanted to do, got on to the adult path two or three years earlier and are forging ahead in their chosen careers, acquiring much valuable, practical experience by the time that the 'graduates', who have (according to your point of view) been either having 'a good time' or struggling desperately to make ends meet, have caught up with them. Equally those who have not been to a university find themselves part of a shrinking pool of suitable employees for businesses which have to choose from unsuitably highly qualified applicants for unsuitably low level skilled jobs.

"The result of the curriculum production process looks like any other modern staple. It is a bundle of planned meanings, a package of values, a commodity whose 'balanced appeal' makes it marketable to a sufficiently large number to justify the cost of production. Consumer-pupils are taught to make their desires conform to marketable values. Thus they are made

How schools impede education

guilty if they do not behave according to the predictions of consumer research by getting the grades and certificates that will place them in the job category they have been led to expect."

[Ivan Illyich *Deschooling Society*]

In her closely argued and scholarly book "*Does Education Matter? Myths about education and economic growth*", Professor Alison Wolf demolishes the received wisdom that prolonged education is at all significantly correlated with economic growth. Rather, it is the other way round; as economies develop, so young people have to compete for jobs in an economy which, as the number of professional jobs grows, increasingly uses credentials for hiring.

"…while this reflects individual self-interest clearly, it is not at all obvious that every extra bit of education is benefiting the economy, or is the best thing on which to spend public money…

"It would be silly to deny the enormous importance of universities as generators of pure ideas, of applications and patents, and of practical industrial consultancy. But, although we may know that our economies need universities, does that mean that they need more of them, or even as many as we have?

"…the percentage of jobs that fall into the 'skilled crafts' categories has fallen steadily throughout the 1980s, and is projected to decline yet more. Moreover, some occupations are thriving which require much less of a 'knowledge base'. The single fastest-growing job of the 1980s was 'postman'; that of the 1990s looks like being 'care assistant' in nursing homes and hospitals – i.e. an essential, low-grade, low-paid and pretty thankless service job. While professional and managerial jobs

Wot, No School?

have certainly exploded in numbers, the greatest shrinkage has been among the skilled and semi-skilled manual jobs in the middle. Low-skilled openings still exist in their millions for people to do things like cleaning streets and offices, packing and delivering boxes, staffing call centres, or operating supermarket checkouts.

"There are all sorts of reasons why more education might benefit people who end up doing jobs like these – but they are not the hard-nosed education-for-growth ones so beloved of contemporary politicians. I find it difficult to construct a convincing argument that more sixth-form qualifications and more degrees are needed so that people will be educated enough to stack shelves, swipe credit cards, or operate a cappuccino machine effectively. And it is important to remember just how many jobs like this do exist, because to listen to a lot of the rhetoric you would think that every semi-skilled or unskilled job was going to vanish tomorrow, if not early this afternoon."

From *Does Education Matter?: Myths about Education and Economic Growth* by Alison Wolf (Penguin Books 2002) copyright © Alison Wolf 2002.

Though there are undoubtedly skills shortages which industry is finding it difficult to fill, industry is on the whole happy to train employees to acquire those specific skills. The specialist skills acquired through higher education are only really needed for specialist jobs e.g. lawyer, doctor, dentist, accountant (though not accounts clerk or bookkeeper) and so on. Many of these, e.g. those required for a solicitor or an accountant can be taught 'on the job'. Employers would be much happier to teach the specialist skills required for their range of jobs, if they knew that their new recruits had the basic skills and attributes listed in Chapter One, rather than finding that though they have a degree they are still without those basic skills which make them immediately employable!

The real difficulty for industry lies in finding potential employees with the necessary general skills of literacy and numeracy and (we suspect) of basic 'social' skills in whom to invest the necessary training. The emergence of a higher percentage of literate, numerate, well-motivated, socially well-adjusted young people from Personal Education, as advocated in Chapter Eight, than currently appear from prolonged 'schooling' may of itself ensure that Britain becomes a more productive country.

If the economic argument for more higher and further education for all has not been made, the prolongation of educational adolescence equally does not seem to bear much fruit in terms of job prospects and career success for large numbers of the graduates of the smaller, less well served universities. For many of those who would employ them there does not seem to have been much gained by those who have had a six year delay between finishing GCSE and beginning on a career path compared with those who have been taking responsibility for their own lives and learning during this time. While published 'life earnings' statistics can currently make a case for investing time and money in a university degree in the expectation of greater financial rewards further down the employment line, what happens when almost everyone has a degree? Will the erosion of the eventual differential make the six, seven, eight year gap such a good investment after all?
With more and more of our young people entering higher education and, if the government has its way,

with well over 50% of them studying for degrees in the near future, the simple premium of a degree has already dropped significantly and the demand for a good graduate job already stands as at least a 2:1 status. Before long the same principle that applied to GCSE results will apply here and only a 1st class degree will be seen as a good degree. Not only that but it will also be seen as a qualification for only certain types of job for which the "problem-based learning" on which A-levels and degrees are currently based is most in demand.

So now, it seems, we are about to do with our universities what we are about to do with our schools, add more and more to our requirements of them. Now we will demand of them that they make up the deficiencies in the schooling system which not only leaves their students without the basic skills in spelling, grammar and arithmetic but without the social or employment skills either.

We should be going in the opposite direction. With a properly balanced schooling for competence as the base and the exploratory years of Personal Education in which to discover and tap into the many and varied talents and skills of many and varied young people, the number of universities can profitably shrink. In part this will simply be formalising the increasing number of closures of unwanted and redundant departments in an increasing number of Higher Education institutions. It may also resurrect the best elements of the underrated Polytechnic system as a natural development of Personal Education. (The Polytechnics weren't academic enough, you see. Since they provided numbers of sub-academic status qualifications that were actually useful to people they didn't fit our image of being suitable for 'good' students. In our image-conscious, style over substance, political and 'educational' world, they had either to go, or to be up-graded to University status, despite the fact that the students didn't want, or need, university-style learning and teaching. No political party wanted to be seen to be closing educational institutions, so upgrading it was the answer; the image became far more glittery and only the learning and the teaching suffered.)

As will be seen in Chapters Seven and Eight, with the 'ladder system' of school education and the freedoms of Personal Education far more of the minority of academically gifted students will be enabled to reach the current levels required for university entrance at a much younger age, particularly in the logical, sequential subjects. This will enable a much smaller number of genuinely academic universities to help develop the capabilities of those young people during the 14 – 16 stage of Personal Education, before admitting the 'brightest and best' into their specialism, some perhaps at 16. For example, there are already fewer universities offering chemistry, or physics, or archaeology, or Arabic, Greek, or Mandarin but in future those that do will attract students who are able to begin degree courses at a far higher starting point than happens now. These universities will have the opportunity to become centres of outstanding excellence, sought after by students from all around the world.

A voluntary dipping in and out of the 'polytechnic' style of further education offered by Personal Education should offer everyone a wide range of academic, practical and creative studies, with many pathways between them as young people define their precise areas of interest and aptitude. The method should offer a

Wot, No School?

combination of the specific knowledge needed within certain occupations, professions or trades, with on-the-job training and experiential learning. In this way it could combine the best of the former Polytechnics and apprenticeships and 'night schools', building on the strong foundations of the School Leaving Certificate and the opportunities of Personal Education.

Flexibility and relevance to interest, skill, talent and aptitude will be the keys. No one would go to a university because the government thinks that they ought. University would be seen as a means to an expansion of the minds which are suited to its nature and style of learning, not as a 'right' nor as a duty nor as a vaguely desirable label to stick on to your c.v.

Chapter Six

The Clean Slate

If at first you don't succeed…. do it again, differently.

We need to escape from the thought-box of 'school', take a clean slate and ask ourselves some fundamental questions: what is best for education, what do we want from it? What is best for learners, what do we want for and from them?

What is best for 'school' doesn't enter into it.

As Prime Minister, Tony Blair declared on the BBC in 2001 that "the key to reform is re-designing the system around the user". Though his government has persisted in redesigning the system around the needs of schools, we agree whole-heartedly that the system should be redesigned with the needs of the learner and of the society that the learner will enter as an adult as the paramount consideration.

At this point we have included a brief outline of the kind of 'clean slate' ideas that might begin to put the needs of twenty first century learning, teachers and individual pupils ahead of the requirements of the nineteenth and twentieth century institutions in which they currently work and the bureaucratic measurers of success and failure. We shall elaborate on these ideas in the next two chapters: Chapter Seven devoted to the 'school' phase of

Wot, No School?

education and Chapter Eight to the post-school 'Personal Education' phase.

We are very aware that we are now entering upon the most dangerous territory in this book. We are confident that many of our readers will have been nodding their heads in agreement with much of what we have had to say about the weaknesses and failings of our current system of schooling - but when it comes to divergent or creative thinking about ways in which to depart from the old and prepare for the new this is the point at which the head shaking and the disagreements will begin.

We are also aware that once we map out some tentative ideas about how we might begin to set about the changes towards a desired educational future, these initial explorations, sketches and suggestions may well be seized upon as our finished articles, our final, complete set of definite proposals. If the UK's recent history of political analysis and commentary is anything to go by, each flaw and blemish however minor (and in any first set of proposals there will be many) that can be ferreted out will be examined minutely, analysed, dissected and held up to ridicule until the big picture is lost and the whole idea is destroyed. Sadly, though the analysers and dissectors could put their particular educated and trained intelligence to an enormously valuable service to all of us, the modern tendency (encouraged, perhaps, by the very analytical, theory-based education these same commentators have received) to take apart but not to seek to improve, may well mean that the initial response of 'I agree with the analysis, but not with the solution' simply leaves us with another pile of rubble and nothing to put in its place, while the destroyers walk away to find something new to pull apart next week. To bend

How schools impede education

Shakespeare: 'As flies to wanton boys are new ideas to the analysts and commentators, They kill us for their sport....' Under the circumstances the temptation is very strong to do what many books such as this one do which is to say, 'This is what's wrong. Here's a list of things which need to be done. We'll leave you to find out how.' – and then to walk away and let someone else get on with it. Probably foolishly we have not succumbed to that temptation, but, probably foolishly, we are about to stick our necks out and wait for the rain of blows to fall!

If all that happens is head shaking and disagreement, if the outcome is simply, "Well, that'll never work" so close the book and go away and do something else, then we will have failed in our purpose. If, on the other hand, the outcome is, "I agree with the general idea but I don't think that'll work. However this might be a better way…" and if we have sparked a debate that leads to a constructive and unified push for change, then we will have at least have had some success. The final success or failure lies with all of us. If we have at least set the ball rolling the future generations of the satisfactorily educated may well have reason to be grateful.

School – Part of the Foundation

Whatever solution we find it will need strong foundations. The first thing, then, is to strengthen the foundations for learning at the early stages of a young person's life.
'Schooling' is part of the foundation for learning.
Groups of young children working with teachers adept at understanding and meeting their needs offer a good way of giving everyone the opportunity to learn how to be a

Wot, No School?

co-operative member of society and of providing the basic essentials for learning.

- ➢ 'School', we suggest, should begin as soon as a child is ready. This might be as soon as three years old or maybe not until six or seven years old.

- ➢ Progress through 'school' could be determined by the child's readiness to move on, not by the child's date of birth. Since not all children progress at the same rate in the same disciplines, children could climb the learning 'ladders' towards a School Leaving Certificate at a rate appropriate to their ability. They probably ought not to begin new ladders until they have climbed securely to the top of the previous ones.

- ➢ There could be a 'School Leaving Certificate', designed to be achievable by the time a child is fourteen. **This Certificate might be the corner stone of such a system**. It would be the hinge between 'school' and 'education'. It would be a certificate of competence, not a measurement of academic achievement.

- ➢ By this means every young person would **earn** the right to leave 'school'. No one should be left as a prisoner of the system, serving out their sentence until they are released simply because they have now become fourteen (or, in the current system, sixteen) years old. With this approach no one would leave 'school' with nothing to show for it, except a clutch of failed exams. Everyone could leave school with their self-esteem boosted by an achievement that would be valued by all of society. Everyone could **earn** the right to choose their own future. Everyone could achieve the most valuable qualification of all, the qualification to take a full part in adult life.

"...an achievement that would be valued by all of society"

➢ We would suggest that anyone who reached, say, their fifteenth birthday unable to pass all the components of the School Leaving Certificate should receive remedial help in those areas where their skills or techniques are deficient, perhaps in a 'school' staffed with specialist teachers.

➢ Such a Certificate should demonstrate that each young person has a sufficient level of literacy and numeracy, and sufficient knowledge of social and cultural institutions, basic law, and basic financial structures to cope constructively with the adult world. This would mean that no one would enter adult society without the knowledge and skills to become a fully independent member of it.

➢ Each component of this rite of passage could be taken when the child is ready.

➢ At the age of fourteen, most, in the areas in which they have the greatest aptitude and interest, could have passed far beyond the Certificate's requirements. For example, a child with strong mathematical or linguistic abilities might well achieve all the necessary requirements for School Leaving Certificate in those areas by the age of eleven or ten, or in some cases even younger. By the time they leave 'school' at fourteen these pupils might have already reached the standards currently required for GCSE, GNVQ, or A-level, or beyond, in those special areas of high aptitude, whether those areas are academic, artistic, cultural, social, technical, practical, scientific… If the young people have the ability to do it, there should be nothing to stop them from doing it.

➢ No one should leave 'school' without the full Leaving Certificate.

➢ After the School Leaving Certificate had been obtained, there need be no further requirement for anyone to go to 'school'.

> However, in order to give everyone a fair chance to discover and develop their own particular skills, talents, and abilities, no one should be employed beyond the limited periods currently allowed for young people until they reach the age of 16.

What we are sketching out is not revolutionary. Much of it is already reflected in those non-academic, non-school areas of learning which depend upon successful outcomes for **participants**, not successful outcomes for the **institutions** which hold them in, and which, in many cases, hold them back.

Personal Education

At age fourteen we are not dealing with toddlers. We should not underestimate what young people, properly equipped and prepared can achieve.

Personal education is the point at which young people can start to take charge of their own learning and take on what has been advocated by Professor John Radford as 'responsible autonomy – the ability to make decisions and take actions, having regard to the interests of others' (*personal communication*). In personal Education, young people would be able to **choose** what they want to learn, academic or otherwise, to whatever level they want to learn it. They would have the chance to take **responsibility** for the learning they do, and for the consequences that would flow from their choices. They would begin the vital lessons of judging what is a mistake and what is success and *learning equally from both.*

> ➢ Between 'school' and employment young people could be **paid** to learn what they are interested in/good at from Personal Education teachers (rather than 'school' teachers) who are interested in/good at it, too.

> ➢ The family could also be 'paid', receiving an element of the learner's total earnings to enable them to support the learner.

> ➢ At age 16 young people might continue Personal Education, enter full time employment, or combine the two.

> ➢ Personal Education teachers could be drawn from a wider range of society – universities, the professions, the business, arts, sporting world and so on – and might find it attractive to be paid as other professionals (doctors, dentists, lawyers, architects etc.) are, through their clients.

> ➢ At the conclusion of the Personal Education stage young people could enter full time employment, or go on to university or to other forms of higher education as they chose and as seemed appropriate to them.

We will deal with the two phases of education summarised above – the 'School' phase and the 'Personal Education' phase in more detail in the next two chapters.

Chapter Seven

How – The School Phase

*...we must attempt to devise an education system which can
cope with the diversity of human needs and interests.
Education must prepare
people for the workplace – and provide employers with
the skills they need – but it must also feed people's
imaginations and enable them to develop their talents
and interests whatever the economic benefit. Education
should also work to create a cohesive and harmonious
society by promoting understanding... thereby giving
much more back to society than society pays in
funding... It is this vision – which includes all and which
responds to the needs of all but which recognizes that
every human being is different – that the education
system today must be able to accept.*

No Child Left Behind – Ibid

We have looked at the problem of an inadequate
education for a large proportion of the population, the
'solutions' that have so far been tried and why they have
not worked.

We have outlined a different solution, which realigns
and replaces the institutions which are holding so many
of our young people and their teachers back. This

solution is based on asking what is education for? rather than what are schools for? It is based on a consideration of what learners and teachers need and the benefits to all members of society, rather than what institutions and bureaucrats need and the benefits to politicians of the current played-out system.

We do not propose to sweep away the whole notion of schooling. Rather we need to recognise the difference between 'schooling' and 'education', apply schooling to the appropriate stage of education and restructure it to give everyone the tools to enter adult life as self-motivated, properly equipped, life-long learners. Many people will tell you that they gained most of their meaningful education after they left school. Sometimes they refer to the 'university of life'. This has so strong a ring of truth about it for so many that it has become a cliché.

For many of those who left school at 16 after O-level or GCSE, or at 18 after A-levels, or obtained degrees from a university, there is a strong sense of someone handing you a certificate or a scroll with a ribbon tied around it with an air of 'congratulations, there's your education done and dusted, nicely wrapped and presented as a well-earned memento for the remainder of your life – now get on and do something real...'

In our proposals 'schooling' exists as the precursor both to that 'university of life', and to the more traditional university of academe. 'Schooling' provides everyone with the skills to begin in life – it is not an end in itself. Leaving school is, in Churchill's words:

How schools impede education

*"...not the end. It is not even the beginning of the end.
But it is, perhaps, the end of the beginning."*
We do not pretend that we have all the questions – let
alone all the answers. We are clear about what we
believe education is for; we are clear that education must
be removed from all party political influence; that
government must become what it is meant to be, the
servant of education for all; that government must realise
that for far too long it has done to education what Philip
Larkin tells us his parents did to him, and leave it to
those people who do know what it is for – the learners,
the teachers, the parents, employers, universities,
professions, services and the disinterested adults upon
whom our society depends.

To reach a solution to the besetting problems of
education among the obstacles we must o'erleap are:

a) the idea that all children and young people must
    always undertake the same academic subjects, for the
    same amount of time, and take the same exams at the
    same age as all other children, regardless of their
    aptitude or ability, or be branded 'failures'
b) the narrow, academically dominated obligatory
    curriculum that excludes as much as it includes or
    more (e.g. physics, chemistry and biology are
    defined as the 'science subjects', while psychology –
    arguably a more useful science for most young
    people – is, for the majority, entirely left out, and
    engineering is set aside for those who can't do
    'proper' science)
c) the insistence that children and young people should
    have little or no choice in what they learn
d) the myopic notion that pupils' individual successes
    are less important than the collective 'success' of the

particular institution they happen to be in and that
their learning should be constricted by the need to
jump through a never ending series of hoops, in the
shape of tests and examinations, in order to measure,
primarily, the success or otherwise of that institution

e) the equally myopic notion that academic ability is of
the greatest good.

This is one way it **might** be done.

The New Schooling – Starting the Beginning

*The direction in which education starts a man will
determine his future life.*

Plato

School should begin when a child is ready for it. No
penalty should be attached to the 'late starter': no
significant advantage need be gained by starting earlier:
the readiness is all.

Ladders

We believe that children should progress through school,
in each learning area, as they become ready for it. No
one should be taken to the next stage until he or she is
well enough equipped to tackle it; no one should be held
back because others have not yet covered the ground;
date of birth or day of year should not be material:
ripeness should be all.

To give a simple example of one way it might be done: -
in a school in which everyone does reading at the same

time in the day every child might become part of the appropriate reading group for their ability; then everyone could go to the appropriate group for arithmetic, then for geography, then for foreign language learning and so on.

Each group could contain the number of pupils who are completing a particular grade or standard, climbing a particular ladder because they can, whatever their chronological age.

We acknowledge that this will present logistical and timetabling problems for schools, but if schools are to be run for the benefit of the learners rather than the administrators… then such difficulties are not insuperable.

Learners

Teachers' views on Pupils

"It's to do with self concept, how you place yourself in society…"
"…'kids' do want to achieve… even those who have written themselves off have a little spark… they can be disaffected in some subjects but not others…" "Low self-esteem and disaffection are closely linked and it's difficult to address."
David Hann: Extracts from M Phil Thesis
Factors Affecting Progression of Students in Thurrock from Secondary into Post 16 Education 2005

Pupils could now learn at a rate which is appropriate to their age, aptitudes and learning styles, not at a rate which has been decreed appropriate to all children by a

Wot, No School?

bureaucrat or educationalist or politician, or at a rate which someone who is unaware of their individual characteristics thinks they 'ought' to be learning.

Currently, the traditional received wisdom of the 'school system' continues to demand that children progress through the system on the basis of chronology, not ability or readiness. The 'ladder' system of learning takes into account the normal stages of brain development in young people. Physical development of the brain is largely completed by the age of 5, but there are subsequent intervals of intellectual development between the ages of 6 and 8, 10 and 12, and 14 and16. There are gender differences to take into account as well. For instance, the natural brain development of girls at age 11 is up to twice that of boys, while something like the converse is true at 15. In our current system of secondary schools it is rare to find a curriculum which takes account of that natural fact. In the system we propose girls may well move faster than boys at this age in some learning areas, but progress up the ladders ensures that each pupil moves up when he or she is mentally, physically, socially and emotionally ready, not when some accident of birth date decrees.

The nay-sayers may well be likely to say at this point that it would be much too difficult to change to a ladder system of advance, rather than the whole-class, chronological system we currently employ. We are not suggesting that it would be easy. However, if that would be the best way ahead for children then it would not be beyond us to bring the very best administrative and organisational brains to bear on the problem, working with the most expert heads and teachers to find the best solution!

How schools impede education

The School Leaving Certificate

All learners, especially as they reach the last three or four years of schooling, should be kept aware of the eventual requirements in basic 'life and learning' knowledge, skills and techniques demanded by the School Leaving Certificate, which should be based on what is essential for anyone to be able to cope competently with the adult world. For the most proficient these requirements might not be, in their areas of high natural proficiency, very demanding. For the least proficient they might well require special help and support to reach the basic standard required before successful pupils can leave school. For example it might not be at all surprising to find youngsters on the one hand producing art and design or engineering work far beyond anything that might be available to them in our current system and on the other attending basic level classes in the essential literacy skills required for competence after 'school': or to find others demonstrating high level skills and expertise in performing arts, or high quality work with wood or metal or plastics, while working overtime in order to achieve the pass certificate in numbers.

Most learners would be likely to move quickly through those areas in which they have strong talents – where things come easily to them, where they can cover the ground comparatively effortlessly. They may complete these elements of the Certificate at a much younger age than 14. Now with the ladder system they would be free, still within their schools, to go with their teachers way beyond the requirements of our current antiquated GCSE or A-level exams, where capable pupils are restrained to often frustratingly low levels by the curious insistence that everyone has to do the same thing as everyone else. Now they could learn with their peers from teachers who are unfettered by the requirements to keep to the pace of the slowest, or to the boundaries of the approved syllabus. In these learning areas they might well be taught in their schools by teachers who also teach at the Personal Education or, in academic subjects, even at the university stage of learning.

The Curriculum

> *Begin with the end in mind*
> Dr. Steven R. Covey – *The Seven Habits of Highly Effective People*,
> Simon and Schuster

The requirements of the 'school' curriculum will spring from the purposes, or the 'end' of schooling – both the preparation for success and the potential for happiness and satisfaction in adult life, and the achievement of the School Leaving Certificate.   Above all it will need to be based on the requirement for every child to achieve competence in the two fundamental skills of literacy and numeracy.

In her book Does Education Matter? (Penguin Books 2002), Professor Alison Wolf makes the point that in an important longitudinal research study of a group of children all born in a particular week of March 1968:-

"The history of the study of participants' lives underscores the enormous importance, in modern society, of basic academic skills. Poor literacy and poor numeracy – especially the latter – have a devastating

How schools impede education

The curriculum will also need to cover a wide range of non-academic as well as academic learning areas. It will need to be strongly focussed on the acquisition of knowledge, skills (including thinking skills) and techniques – the tools needed both for passing the Leaving Certificate and the foundation for future learning in the pupils' areas of aptitude and interest.

As pupils progress through the curriculum by climbing the ladders of knowledge, skill and technique, the ladders could be structured to ensure that all but special cases can reach the Certificate standard by the time they are 14 years old, or very soon after it, though no one should be able to leave school until they have climbed all the Certificate ladders and have demonstrated their proficiency in all the curriculum areas demanded by the full Certificate.

For those pupils who have completed Certificate ladders in any learning area before their 14th birthday, 'Post-Certificate' study could become available. Post-Certificate groups could work within the normal school structure and would generally contain well motivated, interested and capable pupils working as far and as fast as they and their teachers can go. Not all learners would have to continue beyond the Certificate stage in any particular subject, however early they might have reached it. Some pupils might have a facility for the work but no real interest or motivation to go further.

Wot, No School?

Instead, once they have demonstrated their competence to deal with the requirements of adult life in those areas, they would be free to explore new subjects, new ideas with new teachers. Some, as we have seen, might choose to spend more time on their weaker areas in order to ensure that they pass the Certificate by the time they reach the school leaving age. These choices might be facilitated by discussions with a 'free' (tax payer provided) professional mentoring service, as well as with parents, relatives and teachers.

Among those involved in setting and reviewing the Certificated curriculum, could be representatives of the professions, services (social, military, voluntary, civil), industry, business, commerce, engineering, probably universities, never party politicians.

'Certificate' subjects might include such things as:

➤ Reading (including fact and fiction; reading for information, and understanding)
➤ Writing (including stories, accounts, descriptions, play/film or audio scripts, poetry, reports, letters)
➤ Speaking (solo and in a group discussion or debate)
➤ Listening (including speeches, drama, radio, TV/film)
➤ Arithmetic
➤ Measurement
➤ Financial Management (including mortgages, insurance, tax, pensions, income/expenditure)
➤ History
➤ Geography

How schools impede education

- a foreign language, perhaps as a practical spoken experience rather than as an academic study
- Law
- Citizen's Rights and Responsibilities (e.g. including local/regional councils, form filling, jury service)
- Religion (including comparative religion, humanism, agnosticism, atheism etc.)
- Philosophy (including moral issues and thinking skills)
- Biology (including food, diet, medicines)
- Environment (including the impact of human civilisation and its effects etc.)
- Home Management (including power sources & appliances: cooking, cleaning: basic maintenance)
- Information Technology

All of these should be pitched at the level of competence required to enter adult society as independent, thinking individuals.

For example, they should prepare those entering Personal Education to be able to think sufficiently independently and to have acquired sufficient basic knowledge to recognise the difference between truth, fact, opinion, belief, spin and propaganda in advertising, promotion and politics. As adults they should be able to watch an episode of a Television 'News' broadcast, identify any parts that might be classified as 'news' or fact, distinguish between speculation, guess and opinion in the rest, or deduce the political bias of programme makers and newspaper editors and other media folk. Similarly they should give everyone sufficient basic skills and knowledge to cope with the most common

Wot, No School?

vicissitudes of life without having to turn to state or other aid unless they really need it. Employers, too, might require of their employees such basic skills and values as functional literacy and numeracy; responsibility (e.g. understanding the need to turn up on time, every time and being able to do it!); the ability to interact civilly with colleagues/customers/suppliers etc.; the ability to speak clearly on the telephone and take messages accurately; and, perhaps, a modicum of initiative and an ability to ask appropriate questions.

Freed from the narrowing focus of 'league tables', it is individual learners who should be examined, not schools. No longer need there be artificial age or other calendar constraints. Learners could take qualifying tests when they were ready to do so. The curriculum would be driven by the learning needs of individuals and the whole range of the society which they wish to enter.

Within the 'non-Certificate' curriculum all children could be introduced to Art, Craft, Drama, Music, all the national sports and games and a variety of activities involving teamwork, organisational and leadership skills. All these and all other subjects to which all pupils might be introduced, such as Algebra, Architecture, Chemistry, Environmental studies, Geometry, Greek, History, Latin, Physics, Politics, Textiles, etc. could, if required by the pupil and recommended by the teacher, be taken further and could receive certificates of achievement. However the main purpose would be to open learners' eyes to the richness of possibilities that exist in future learning and to give them a chance to discover whether they have an inclination, an interest or an aptitude for them, not to examine the pupils in order to offer evidence of success or failure for the measurers.

How schools impede education

Music/Drama/Gymnastics grade examinations might continue as before. Other games and sports e.g. Athletics, Canoeing, Cricket, Football, Hockey, Orienteering, Rugby, Sailing, Tennis, etc. etc. might devise their own award system to recognise achievement and encourage improvement, for those who wish to take them, if they were considered beneficial or motivational.

As children reached the age of 11 they would be approaching the last three years of 'school'. The Leaving Certificate would begin to figure more strongly in their lives.   As the Personal Education phase of learning draws near now might be the time for them to meet, if they choose, professional mentors whose role would be to guide them towards and through the decisions and challenges ahead.

Mentors

Teacher's views on Mentoring

"Year 8 mentoring works really well and gets kids to think more long-term..."
"To let them know there are FE options for all, to make them feel less excluded... ask them 'what do you see yourself becoming' etc."
"Tutorials are changing from focus on the past to what you are going to do in the future."
David Hann: *Extracts from M Phil Thesis*

At the age of around 14 pupils who have completed their School Leaving Certificate would become free to pursue Personal Education. There could be a multiplicity of options and a multiplicity of learning providers from whom they could choose. No longer would they need to have any kind of set curriculum which they are bound to follow. No longer need their hours be fixed by a school timetable. No longer need there be a single, unchanging place of work.

The transformation from total dependence on a school system to the beginnings of complete self-reliance would be a potentially thrilling moment in their rite of passage into the adult world. However, if many young people were to be suddenly left entirely to their own devices, the transition could be not merely dramatic, but traumatic. A 'free', state-provided mentoring service could be made available to everyone and might become central to many in the successful exploration of such a boundless educational environment.

The role of a mentor could be exactly what the name implies: one who is an independent, uncritical guide and source of information. As such, it would probably be better if mentors were not teachers, nor employees of the school system, but members of an independent profession, appropriately trained and qualified. Mentors could act as sounding boards for young people's ideas, aspirations, difficulties, needs and desires and take the part of those who help turn these aspirations and needs into achievable goals and pathways. Mentoring would be available when each child is ready which, for the vast majority, would not be before the age of eleven. By that age quite a large proportion would have already exceeded the requirements of the Certificate in one or more areas and will be beginning to make choices about what they wish to do in the time thus 'freed'.

How schools impede education

Any mentor who said "You couldn't possibly do that" should be instantly dismissed.

Teachers

Many, perhaps most teachers, especially our current primary school teachers, might choose initially to remain 'school' teachers, teaching young people up to the age of 14 at schools in Pre-Certificate or Post-Certificate groups, or both, as their skills and inclinations took them.

Some Personal Education and university teachers might also choose to engage in 'Post Certificate' teaching within schools, engaging with bright, young, comparatively 'untutored' minds which can produce startling insights.

This approach to teaching would not only bring new teachers into the schools but enable existing teachers to expand their horizons. For instance, if they wished to remain within the 'school' structure but specialize in Post-Certificate teaching (as some teachers in the current system specialise in GCSE and A-level teaching) they might not need to teach all the time, every day. They might not have only to teach in school. If they chose, they could also teach at the post-school Personal Education stage or they could apply their other skills, aptitudes and interests to a working life outside the school walls for part of the day, or part of the week – or they could take time out of their school teaching career for a number of years to pursue a particular interest, or to learn new skills, or to fulfil an ambition. They would have the same chance as everyone else for variety in

Wot, No School?

their working lives and their adult experience. Their gift for teaching could, if they wished, be kept fresh, along with their enthusiasm, by a number of contrasting experiences.

After each element of the Leaving Certificate was completed, the absence of the necessity to get everyone 'through the exam' in time, would free teachers from the demands of 'teaching for the exam' and allow them to concentrate on the real and differing needs of groups and individuals as they met them. There would be no 'league tables' to massage for the benefit of the institution, only learners who needed and wanted to learn, either with a compelling extrinsic motivation to reach the required standard or an even more compelling intrinsic motivation to explore, or to advance, or to prepare for Personal and life Education.

Though Post-Certificate learning for those pupils who had not yet completed the full Certificate could take place in the normal structures and environment of 'school', it could leave the confines of a 'compulsory for all' syllabus and could travel as far and as fast, as wide and as deep as the learners and teachers could take it, both for those who might wish to go on to study an academic subject at university or in Personal Education, and for those who were pursuing an interest or fascination for its own sake.

Those teachers whose skill and vocation it is to serve young people who struggle, for intellectual, academic, social or emotional reasons, would not only still be required in schools but, vitally, could be given the time in which to enable those pupils to reap the rewards of their efforts. Pupils who find it hard to climb some of the

How schools impede education

learning ladders securely would not be compelled to wobble uncertainly up them, missing out vital rungs in the haste to beat the age deadline, or to take meaningless interim tests and exams to prove how well the school is conforming to government requirements. For many of these young people the single goal of the competence Certificate would enough. Given the time and the skilled support of specialist teachers their chances of reaching it would be hugely enhanced, even as they roared ahead with other teachers in the areas where their natural aptitudes were free to flourish. As all parents and teachers know, success in one area enhances the possibilities for success in other areas – provided that success is recognised and valued as success, not devalued because it isn't the 'right kind' of success.

In the case of the current system the 'right kind' of success is, almost invariably, success in academic subjects, though sporting, artistic, dramatic or musical success may gain some applause, especially if they are associated with money or 'celebrity'. In the system we envisage achievement, effort and success, from all learners and all teachers, could be recognised and valued for what they were, wherever they occurred.

The process of *schooling* which we have sketched out above could give all our young people the chance to begin the process of *education*, equipped with the skills and the knowledge which lead to what Professor John Radford has summarised as *'responsible autonomy'*. Initiated into the traditions of the society's knowledge, they could now begin the challenging adventure towards, in Professor James Tooley's words, *'personal empowerment'* through what we describe as 'Personal Education'.

Chapter Eight

How 2 – Personal Education

A fundamental goal of education for adult life and personal empowerment should be the transition of the control of learning from teachers to pupils.

Once pupils have completed all the parts of the curriculum that are required for the School Leaving Certificate, they could be free to do just that – leave school and begin their Personal Education. Guided, perhaps by professional mentors if they chose, and by their families, they could begin to find their own pathways, explore their potential, learn skills which develop their natural talents to higher, more satisfying levels and acquire knowledge which attracts and interests them as they prepare for either the academic, or the 'life' university, where learning never stops.

Structure

"...healthy students often redouble their resistance to teaching as they find themselves more comprehensively manipulated. This resistance is due ... to the fundamental approach common to all schools – the idea that one person's judgement should determine what and when another person must learn."

[Ivan Illyich *Deschooling Society*]

How schools impede education

School's out! (or, at least, I'm out of school!)

Once pupils have passed all the elements of the School Leaving Certificate, they would not need to go to *school* – ever again. Instead, they could go to *teachers* to learn what they wanted or needed to learn – or they could decide not to. They could begin the process of learning 'responsible autonomy', by choosing to go for Personal Education – or choosing not to.

Personal Education could be available to anyone who wanted it. Once the full Leaving Certificate had been obtained, would-be learners could be provided with a list of all the Post-Certificate, Personal Education teachers, with the range of all the areas for study offered, who could be found in their neighbourhood or through distance learning using advancing technology. If they chose to visit one of the professional mentors, a service which could be provided by the state as part of the Personal Education programme, they could receive more practical, focussed advice about the possibilities that awaited them.

Schooling, in our method, would be for competence, education would be for life enhancement. If 'school' education itself is to be more concerned with laying the foundations for thinking and understanding, with developing creativity, ideas, belief, knowledge and with acquiring the tools, techniques and skills of abstract thinking – analysis, recording, enquiring, hypothesising, drawing conclusions, distinguishing fact from opinion, generating new ideas, thinking up different solutions, planning, making decisions, and so on – then Personal Education might also include more of the element of training.

Wot, No School?

In Personal Education young people might begin to get the chance to use their own judgement, to make their own choices as to which specific skills and techniques they wished to develop, to realise those ideas of particular interest and attraction to them, to solve specific problems, address specific tasks or types of task, to apply their knowledge. Pupils who discovered and developed a natural academic interest and aptitude at school might well wish to spend a considerable portion of their Personal Education time on academic learning, partly for its own sake and partly to discover whether they wished to embark in due course on a university degree. Obviously, the opportunity would be there for the universities to make degree study much more rigorous, since they would have the opportunity to admit academically inclined students who have been working with equally able and motivated peers under teachers who have had far more chance to challenge them beyond the confines of the current syllabuses. Such students, emerging from self-chosen academic Personal Education would be likely to be far further advanced in their learning than the current crops of A-level qualified students. Of course, university entry need not be the sole reason for pursuing academic subjects in Personal Education. Other pupils might pursue them for their own sake, simply because they interested and challenged and satisfied them, others might study them for 'vocational' reasons because they wished to enter medicine, or the law, or scientific research, or engineering, or technology either instead of immediate employment or in parallel with it.

It is probable that, given the opportunity to exercise their own judgement and pursue their own interest and aptitudes, far fewer young people would wish to confine themselves to academic study alone, or even to engage upon academic study at all beyond the School Leaving Certificate. For instance, though one young person might want to develop thinking skills and techniques for problem solving in different forms of practical or theoretical sciences, another might want to develop manual or visual skills and techniques for botanical illustration or for design and realisation in mechanics and another might want to find out more about the skills and techniques required for manufacturing, running their own business or for marketing and selling new ideas. As a consequence there might be teachers of art and accountancy, physics and photography, of electrical engineering and economics, of baking or business practices, of presentation graphics, programming, public speaking, catering, demographics, administration... There might be courses in plumbing and mechanical engineering, in information technology and design, in architecture and literature, in sports sciences and in sports skills, in retailing and machine tooling, in pipe laying and shop fitting, in anything and everything where there was a demand and a supply, learners to learn and teachers to teach.

If we are truly interested in developing the life chances for all then there might also be an opportunity for the worlds of business and industry to offer courses which would help young people to develop the skills of which they believe they are most in need. For instance in the spring of 2006 a number of the major businesses in the UK were asked by the Council for Industry and Higher Education what they most wanted in a new recruit. The most common answers were 'innovation' and the 'ability to think creatively'. Personal Education might give them the chance to give young people the chance to develop precisely those skills they most require.

The bulk of learners undertaking Personal Education might be fourteen or fifteen year olds fresh from the Leaving Certificate. However, perhaps increasingly as the method developed, there also might be older students brushing up on skills or knowledge for a change in course or to provide themselves with new career options, or adults re-training, or simply those who wished to find out that there was more to life than they currently knew and to continue the process of life-long learning and self-discovery. Flexibility for learners and teachers would be the key to Personal Education.

A significant element of that flexibility could be that young people would no longer need to be confined to the same group of teenagers with whom to work in the same place for almost every lesson of almost every day of almost every week, during the same strictly defined hours and terms, for the next two or three years. Under the current system of secondary schooling we corral groups of often reluctant, frequently disaffected teenagers throughout the GCSE years, compelling them all to do what many of them don't want to do (and arguably don't need to do), are not interested in doing and in many cases have little aptitude for and little chance of real success in, with companions they have not chosen and for purposes that may well be unclear as well as unwinnable, and are certainly not their own. It is hardly surprising that this system exacerbates disaffection, nor is it in the least surprising that it is in this age group especially that rates of school 'exclusions', of truancy and other forms of social disruption rise rapidly.

How schools impede education

On the other hand, as indicated above, since Personal Education 'classes' might include a wide range of learners, all with the common bond of an interest in and a desire or need to learn in the area of study or training, young people could benefit extraordinarily by working alongside older learners, especially if those people are already in employment and aware of the clear advantages to themselves in their careers of the learning they are undertaken. The apprentice system has for centuries shown that this maturity of perspective rubs off on the younger learners and can produce remarkable changes in attitude with consequent changes in outcomes to their learning.

Similarly, there would no longer need to be set 'exam' months or times of year to dictate who needs to be in school, when, and for how long. Personal Education could provide another bridge towards full adult life simply because there would no longer be the need in this age group for 'school terms' and 'school holidays'. This is precisely the age at which youngsters no longer want to go on holiday with the rest of the family, but with everyone out of school at the same time, parents are often condemned to dragging along reluctant, sulking teenagers who don't want to come with the rest of the family but can't be left behind to spend aimless, idle weeks at home in the company of no one, or in the company of other equally purposeless drifters with nothing to occupy them. We all know that these idle hands make perfect tools for many social devils.

We also know of the herds of adolescents, surging and drifting around our streets, shops, recreation grounds, parks and waste lands at fixed periods of the year for two or three weeks at a time and for far longer in the summer, with 'nothing to do' and 'nowhere to go', seeking for amusement and without the wherewithal to find it or, more importantly, create it. The frustration and boredom engendered frequently breaks out in the form of vandalism, anti-social behaviour, sometimes into apparently motiveless petty crime or violence. However, during Personal Education teachers and course organisers would be arranging courses to suit a whole range of requirements of place and time, as well as of a variety of learners of different ages. Since the youngsters involved would be motivated wage earners taking responsibility for their own attendance, there would be at least the potential to remove another running sore from social life not just for parents and adolescents but for everyone else as well.

Earning Learners

Though employment legislation could still prevent anyone aged between 14 and 16 from entering any other form of employment for any more hours in a day, or in a week, than is currently permitted, there need be no *obligation* on anyone to do any further learning once they had the full Certificate. However, those who did choose to continue learning could be *paid* to do it. This need not come as a completely revolutionary idea. After all we are already paying several thousand young people to stay on at school in different parts of the country!

At the same time, all forms of Child Benefit, Child Tax Credit or any other kind of state support for the family of a school leaver could cease. A proportion of what each young person earned for attending classes with a teacher could then be paid directly to the family. The more

How schools impede education

learning time, the more pay the teenager would earn –
though it might be advisable, particularly in the early
stages, to set some kind of limit to avoid the temptation
for some to exploit the earning potential of the young
learner for their own ends. Learning 'wages' might be
set with an eye to the Minimum Wage that is in
operation at the time, with a proportion being paid to the
family, a greater share to the wage earner and a similar
share paid directly to the teacher whose lessons the
young person attended. As well as the financial benefit
to the family there would be great benefits to the sense
of responsibility and the self esteem of the teenage
learners, who would become contributors to the well
being of the whole family through their own efforts.

At 16 young people could, as they could at the start of
the twenty first century, go into full employment – or
they could continue Personal Education, for one, two,
three more years, or right up to a degree qualification.
Throughout this period they could continue to be paid
for a certain number of hours of study per week. Once
they reached the age of 16 they might supplement their
learning wage with other part-time employment, just as
students have always done. Naturally, they could
become subject to taxation once their earnings took them
beyond the Personal Allowance, just as any other worker
is.

Some young people might not achieve the School
Leaving Certificate so soon. For those who had not
achieved it by the time they were 15, their ability to
survive effectively in the adult world would be in doubt.
At this point they could go to highly focused schools,
staffed with specialist teachers, in order to achieve their
Certificates. Some of these schools might be boarding

schools: some might be staffed with specialists in various forms of learning difficulties. The aim of all of them would be to enable the young people referred to their care to acquire the basic skills and knowledge to join the working world with a fair opportunity for success and for employment. The pupils in these schools might, as 'school' pupils, not be paid for learning, though the state would continue to support their families through Family Tax Credit or whatever other system replaced it. These factors of compulsory 'school' and lack of income, compared to their now 'free' and wage earning former school fellows, would be strong incentives for the merely idle, or the disaffected or the stubborn, to pass the Leaving Certificate as soon as they could.

Some young people might opt to do no formal work or learning in the years between achieving the Leaving Certificate and becoming of an age to enter full time employment. They might come from families sufficiently wealthy and sufficiently indulgent not to need any income nor to be made to do any work. The state, once it had ensured that they had achieved the right to leave school through their Certificate, would be relieved of any obligation to support them financially.

Some of these 'opters out' (whether temporary or permanent), all of whom would have the basic skills and knowledge to take part in the adult world, might be the eccentrics, the adventurers, the entrepreneurs, the original thinkers, who had the good fortune to be free to carve out their own idiosyncratic paths to a destiny that might change the way the rest of us live. Others might simply be idle, pampered scions of wealthy and indulgent homes – spiritual descendants of the land-

How schools impede education

owning aristocracies of the past and fated to aimless, parasitic lives, the Bertie Woosters of our time. At least they would create no financial burden on the state, since they would not qualify for any of the benefits applicable to those who work, and they would make a net contribution to the economy through the money they spent. Others might be people who were late developers, awaiting their Damascene moment before surprising us all. Others might be, as they have been throughout the last century, victims of a criminal environment, lured by the prospect of 'easy money' through drug dealing or other forms of criminal activity, to a life of crime and probable imprisonment. (The fact that, unlike a high proportion of the 20th century prison population, all 'school leavers' would be basically literate and numerate might help many to avoid this fate.)

Only a totalitarian regime seeks to impose an educational system which reduces everyone to the same 'Brave New World' state of approved compliance. In a free society, education recognises the richness and diversity of human beings and does its best to prepare and forearm its young people against the whole range of foreseeable possibilities, without seeking to mould them into what its political or other leaders think is 'best for them'. What matters is that no emerging citizen should lack a basic education, and everyone should have the same educational chance to advance in the most appropriate way from that same base line.

Curriculum

Wot, No School?

Teachers' views on the current curriculum

"The syllabus restricts kids... they're not motivated by GCSEs, need more hands on stuff..."
...need a better balance between life skills and qualifications..."
"The problem is that schools need to produce GCSE results... people only look at league tables..."
"Disaffection is worst in Years 10 and 11... they need an alternative timetable... and outdoor pursuits and college courses..."
"...emphasis on exams tends to undermine some who are short of skills."

David Hann: *Extracts from M Phil Thesis*

In Personal Education the curriculum could comprise every area of human skill, aptitude, curiosity or interest where there is a learner to learn and a teacher to teach.

There need be no arbitrary 'value' system, no entrenched attitude that academic study is 'worth' more than non-academic study, no attempt to make pointless equations between essentially non-comparable learning areas.

Carl: If you ask me, Mohammed Ali in his prime was much better than anti-lock brakes.
Lennie: Yeah, but what about Johnny Mathis versus Diet Pepsi?

The Simpsons

What would matter would be ability, effort and achievement. What would matter would be successful learning. What would matter would be good teaching. In Personal Education those who wished to study 'academic' subjects could opt-in to studying them.

How schools impede education

Those who wished to pursue other skills, or develop different techniques could opt-in to those.

To ensure that learners did not narrow too quickly into specialist areas, there might be a requirement for those who seek payment from tax payers for their studies initially to devote a proportion of their learning week to each of a number of more general areas of learning.

As a starting point for debate, general learning areas, perhaps for the first year after completion of the School Leaving Certificate, might comprise:
- Aesthetic/Cultural (art, dance, drama, film, history, music, painting, photography, writing …)
- Creative (cabinet making, cooking, design, fashion, film making, furniture, hair styling, musical composition/performance, photography, theatre, writing…)
- Physical – Outdoor (athletics, camping, canoeing, climbing, cycling, Duke of Edinburgh Award, exploration, fishing, games, orienteering, Outward Bound, riding, walking…)
- Teamwork, Co-operative (community projects, team games, musical/dance/theatrical productions, Young Enterprise…)
- Technical/Scientific (agriculture, botany, chemistry, electronics, engineering, information technology, mechanics, physics, plumbing, wiring…)

In the second year after completion of the Certificate another area might be added:
- Service (community service, gardening, helping with young children, visiting and helping out the

old or infirm, scouting, Sea Cadets, St John's
Ambulance service ...)

Learning in the general Aesthetic, Creative and
Scientific areas might, or might not be academic,
depending on the interests and aptitudes, aims and
ambitions of the learner. No one would have to study
any academic subjects at all, though everyone would
have to take part in non-academic work in the Physical
and Teamwork areas of the wage earning curriculum.

No learning area need be accorded a higher or lower
status than any other. All that would matter would be its
value and suitability to the aspirations or the enrichment
of the learner, and the greater breadth it would give to
them as they encountered the possibilities of a full adult
life. The effort, application, perseverance, persistence
and achievement of the learners would be the most
highly prized by the society they are preparing to enter.

Qualifications

Some, though not all, areas of study or training
undertaken in Personal Education might lead to
qualifications, but only where qualifications would be
considered appropriate or even necessary - just as no one
needs a qualification to ride a bicycle, only the ability to
do it, but training and qualifications for car drivers, and
for drivers of buses or heavy goods vehicles, or trains, or
aeroplanes are necessary and provided by the appropriate
licensing bodies. There would be no qualifications for
the sake of qualifications, no need to wave pieces of
paper, where no one other than a bureaucrat or a

government measurer, is interested in the piece of paper you wave.

Academic qualifications might be largely provided by universities, professional qualifications by the professions involved. Civil service qualifications could be decided by the civil service; military qualifications by the military; engineering qualifications by the Institutes of Engineering; teaching qualifications by the Teaching Council; coaching qualifications, if required, by the sporting body which requires them; banking qualifications by banks.

There need be no arbitrary standard set by people who are removed from the body which requires them for any of these qualifications. Like the learning and the teaching which precedes them, each qualification would be valuable, necessary and focussed upon the needs of the employers or the members of the profession of the awarding body.

Motivated learners

Earlier in the book we listed some of the things that are desirable for successful learning: guidance as to how to learn; the tools for independent learning; ownership of meaningful knowledge; optimism – the knowledge that you have a real chance to succeed; hope – based on the experience of previous success; the expectation of success; encouragement to success; motivating, empathetic, skilled and knowledgeable teachers; the creation of the best conditions for learning; permission to fail; and good reasons for trying again.

Wot, No School?

Pre-Certificate learning would clearly need to be based on these desiderata while Post Certificate Personal Education could build on them.

Personal Education would provide both extrinsic and intrinsic motivation for all learners. Extrinsic motivation would come, in part, from tangible, financial reward, both to the learner and the learner's family, responding to the degree of effort put in. It would also spring from the freedom to choose your own goals and targets: to choose areas of learning, whether non-academic or academic, which developed your particular skills, aptitudes and interests towards a potentially rewarding and satisfying working future. It would stem, too, from the clear knowledge and understanding that future employers or universities might well want to study your Personal Education record before making, or not making you an offer.

A more powerful intrinsic motivation would include the interest generated by a learning area which you had chosen for yourself, because it was what you wanted to do, and by the greater likelihood of success in areas where you have not just the interest but also the skills and the aptitude, rather than in those into which you were pitch-forked regardless because everybody had to do them. That intrinsic motivation would have every chance to be refreshed by the achievement of personal goals and stimulated by meeting challenges which you believed would satisfy you and which you were confident of surmounting. For many of our young people, unlike those who once laboured without receiving a proper respect for their abilities in the previous 'academic-based' system, much personal motivation could be generated simply from the

How schools impede education

knowledge that the society in which you were taking your first individual steps sufficiently valued whatever you were learning and your efforts and successes in learning it to pay you to do more of it!

Two fundamental characteristics that are found in successful learners everywhere are high expectations and high self-esteem. People are not born with positive or negative self-images. The image young people have of themselves is one they have learned. In the current 'school' system some learn early or late that they are destined for failure, that the academic work that everyone insists is the only work that really matters, is 'unwinnable'. Many bright young people quickly realise that the best way to avoid losing is not to enter – 'You've got to be in to lose', so don't go in. Such image making can be changed, but the longer it is left the more ingrained it becomes. We believe that if pre-Certificate learning established early on every learner's strengths, demonstrated to everyone what they *could* do rather than what they *couldn't*, then during Personal Education, with their self-esteem already raised by their success in qualifying to join the adult world, higher levels of expectation would come from the learners themselves. The debilitating and disruptive effects of boredom, so often seen in those pupils who were condemned to pursuing 'school subjects' in which and for which they had neither interest nor aptitude, would no longer be tolerated by them.

Some Personal Education learners might have their sense of personal worth further supported by employment, or 'sponsorship' by businesses or services or universities in the form of scholarships, or as part of their training entitlement within the career structure of an organisation. The majority, who might wish to keep all their options open, would have every encouragement to value their potential contributions to society simply by the open wish of teachers to teach them and by the interest shown in their choices as well as in their progress by the other influential adults in their lives.

As we noted earlier, the last major interval of intellectual development occurs during the Personal Education phase, between the ages of 14 and 16. During this stage there is an enormous re-organisation of the physical brain, involving changes in its structure and growth which affect its day to day functioning. Almost all parents know of the phenomenon of the previously eager, biddable, up-with-the-lark-child, who becomes almost overnight the morose, mood changing, late sleeping, introspective, rebellious, Neanderthal figure – the Kevin of our nightmares, for long and often unpredictable periods unwilling to reason (unless it suits, when every form of self-advantaging argument pours out in a largely incoherent, emotionally confused and logically irrefutable *ragout* of the rational and irrational) and with almost no notion of planning ahead, foreseeing or understanding the consequences of actions ("It's not my fault. I didn't know that it would just break like that... that he wouldn't like ..."). Erratically occurring phases of bewildering rebellion (often as bewildering to the adolescent as to the adult) against everything that was previously taught and accepted are often accompanied by a highly emotional and almost entirely un-thought-out demand to learn everything for themselves and an expectation that, though their parents are stupid, ignorant, embarrassing and downright obstructive thwarters of their every aim or passion they

How schools impede education

will nonetheless continue to provide the wherewithal to satisfy every whim.

In the old days, school, with its timetables, its clocks, its bells, its herding corridors and restraining adults compelling the adolescent to do things which for very many were mainly pointless and unwinnable and there for the purposes of other, distant adults rather than the pupils and their teachers, exacerbated the downside of the condition and allowed very little outlet for the questing, adventuring, risk-taking turbulence of unusual thought processes, very little chance to learn from self-regulation, choice, trial and, above all, error. In school things had to be 'done this way, because…' – perfect ammunition for the often idealistic young mind which resisted every 'because', often recognising the insincerity of a 'because' which was the 'because' of someone else, not the teacher who wearily deployed it.

Personal Education might not offer the learner a perfect world, but it would at least offer the opportunity to choose, to direct your own path, take your own consequences, acquire a set of personal responsibilities, make mistakes and learn from them, find out what you can do, rather than what you can't, and achieve positive rewards for getting it right, rather than negative strictures for getting it wrong.

Mihaly Csikszentmihalyi, a psychologist from Chicago, noted that young people who do best in the transition to adult life are usually those who took most responsibility for their lives and their learning during their adolescence. Personal Education would offer everyone the chance to take this same advantage.

Wot, No School?

Teachers, old and new

Many teachers might, initially, wish to remain within the Pre Certificate school structure, teaching as they do now but not to GCSE or A-level taking classes. Teachers who opt for Personal Education might find it satisfying to achieve fully recognised professional status by belonging to a professional body which would be responsible for their training, accreditation and registration. They might not be required to have university degrees, unless a university degree would be appropriate for the material or subject which they wished to teach. Nor would they have to undergo years of training in the history and approved methods of pedagogy. The requirement might simply be for them to demonstrate a comprehensive grasp of the material they intended to teach and an ability to teach it successfully to a wide range of those who wished to learn it. In addition none of them would have to be 'only' a teacher, none of them would have to be a teacher for life, none of them would have to teach in a school, none of them would have to be full time.

In this way more and more adults might become involved, in however small a way, in passing on their skills and knowledge and experience to a new generation. The possibility of this kind of teaching could become attractive as well as satisfying to a much larger number of people. It might return to them something of that missing sense of worth and purpose, the feeling that what you do is not just worthwhile, but worth passing on, and ease some of the restlessness, dissatisfaction and malaise we recognise as a growing phenomenon of the early twenty first century. With a lifestyle which includes the loss of the extended family and all the possibilities of enrichment which that entailed, the opportunities for a much wider range of teachers might help with the creation of a virtuous circle of learning, bringing the generations into a more meaningful relationship with one another. It might also make it easier for the potentially disaffected young learner to recognise that learning is not just something that is done at 'school' and teaching is not just something that is done by school-teachers but is part of the whole process of advancement in life.

Some of the full time professional teachers in Personal Education might be teachers of academic subjects, others might be instructors or trainers in practical, applied skills and techniques. 'Part time' teachers might be engaged in the 'non-teaching' world of work as employed technicians, researchers, designers, craftsmen, artists, photographers, entrepreneurs, copywriters, salesmen, managers, engineers, hairdressers, receptionists, draughtsmen, manufacturers, agricultural/transport/utility worker. As we have suggested, such people might be drawn to teaching by a personal interest in education, or they might be volunteers, 'seconded' to teaching by socially responsible businesses, or organisations which have a positive interest in the advancement of education. Some of them might be young people, encouraged by their employers to learn teaching skills and to develop their own knowledge and understanding through teaching others, as part of their career structure. Others might be older people, nearing retirement and glad to pass on their knowledge and expertise to those who are starting out.

All of them could bring to their teaching and to their students a knowledge and experience of the adult working world, its current techniques, ideas and practices. In many cases they would offer a relationship more nearly that of the master/apprentice or the teacher/disciple. That relationship has proved immensely fruitful in so many cultures all over the world and throughout time but has become increasingly difficult for the modern, specialist school teacher, who has spent many years being trained in the art of school teaching, with little opportunity to experience the world outside 'school'. Of itself it could become another small factor in re-building the sense of responsibility to one another and to the generations that we seem to be increasingly losing in the gathering pace and frenzy of our whirligig of time.

Some Personal Education teachers might work independently. Some might work together in teams or co-operatives, like barristers in chambers with clerks to handle the administration, or doctors or dentists in surgeries with receptionists, or solicitors in firms with secretaries. Some teachers might be employed by a learning provider, an organisation collecting fees, and dealing with administration and resources: many might be employed by industry, businesses or professions, seeking to raise the skill levels of would-be applicants. Some of these might utilise parts of the former secondary or further education buildings no longer required or only partly required during the day by the Certificate teaching schools. Some might work from offices, or studios or from their own homes. Some might be employed, perhaps in the afternoons and evenings when the 'school' children have gone home, by sponsoring bodies such as universities, the armed services, businesses, or professional bodies committed to the advancement of learning, some of which might build their own specialist premises for the purpose.

Those teachers who were not directly employed by a learning provider, or by a business or industry, could earn their salaries from the proportion of the 'wage' paid by the state to each individual learner, which would be allocated to their teacher. They could make their own decisions not only about what they taught but where they taught, how often they taught, and how many pupils they taught.

Some of the old secondary school organisations, particularly those with good technological, sporting or other facilities might continue to use the buildings and the facilities as before, offering a complete service of accommodation, administration, catering and accounting to a range of learners and teachers engaged in Personal Education. Many might specialise in offering employment to teachers of academic, technical, sporting, musical, dramatic or artistic subjects. Students attending these 'compendium' learning providers would still need to fulfil all of the broadening areas of the curriculum if they, and through them their teachers, were to qualify for pay. They could still retain the choice of what they wanted to learn and they might not have to take all their studies with this one learning provider. In some cases these 'compendium' providers might employ teachers directly, in others they might charge teachers rent for the accommodation, facilities and services they offered.

Wot, No School?

Kids' current views on teachers

"They gang up on you and make you learn what you don't want to…"
"We don't think in posh terms like they do."
"Prefer to learn, but it should be interesting… which is not very often."
"Don't really say much [but encourage you] to concentrate on exams, do well in GCSEs and SATs to get you into college."
"They think we aren't going anywhere. [They think I'll be] an illiterate dustman."
"Never talk one-to-one."

David Hann: *Extracts from M Phil Thesis*

For teachers engaged in Personal Education perhaps the strongest intrinsic motivation would be teaching something you love and are good at to pupils who love it and want to be good at it, too. Since there would be no compulsion to force reluctant pupils to endure what they had neither interest in nor aptitude for, the comparative ease of keeping pupils motivated and interested, inspired and enthused would have every chance to keep teachers equally refreshed, and stimulated, too.

In helping to maintain an appropriate focus to the teaching and learning an independent, professional organisation might not only monitor standards of teaching and the professional behaviour of teachers on behalf of pupils, parents and future employers, but also provide support and advice and opportunities for further training where required. Such a 'teaching standards' organisation should properly be funded by the taxpayers. Perhaps elected representatives of the tax paying, interested parties, on whose behalf it did the monitoring, might lead and drive the board of directors, but political parties should be legally barred from interference in its working.

Employment and enjoyment

Once children had passed the essential School Leaving Certificate, which would itself ensure they had the basic 'academic' and 'social' skills, they would be far more likely to come closer to 'fulfilling their potential' than by being drilled through the academic hoops of GCSEs and A-levels as happens now. With basic literacy, numeracy and social skills, and a track record of thorough Personal Education, they would, at least, have attractive employment potential to an employer who might be happy to invest training in the specific skills, be they manual, clerical or inter-personal, required for a particular job. The habit of only selecting employees from over-qualified graduates, because they are available and because their higher education makes them more likely to have the much more important credentials of cognitive and motivational abilities than the disaffected who left school with nothing to show for it would, perhaps, gradually die away.

As we have reiterated throughout this book, education is not only for successful employment. It is for the fulfilment of life. We all carry what Alan Bennett calls the weightless baggage of acquired knowledge and skills that we leave unused from one year to the next. Our hobbies and interests, the snatches of songs or poems, the good jokes, the films we have seen, the stories we have heard, the objects we have made, the places we have visited may now be quite useless to our *employment*, but they are essential to our *enjoyment* in social intercourse, in life beyond employment, in our personal satisfaction, happiness and effectiveness as parents, friends or relatives or employees. If Personal Education could carry the young person just that little bit further than they ever seriously thought that they could go; if it could open doors that they never even knew existed let alone those they thought were permanently closed to them; if it could reveal that hard work can be in *itself* a more pleasurable activity than dedicated self-indulgence then it would have done a great deal more for a huge percentage of our young people than all the hours wasted in learning, not a subject, but *how to pass an exam* in a subject.

Chapter Nine

How Will It Work?

In this chapter we attempt to summarise the ideas already outlined, under the heading 'signposts' show how many of the ideas are already being tried out (albeit always in the context of an institution, gripped by central government control and interference) as more and more educators try to find ways round the shortcomings of the current academic straightjacket. Finally, we pose a number of questions where we feel that either our suggestions are too sketchy and require more detail or where, perhaps there may be other, better solutions. We do this in the hope that you, our thoughtful readers, will be able to design better metaphorical mousetraps by writing to debate@wotnoschool.com

The Summary

The 'School' part of education should begin when each child is ready for it. This will depend upon a number of factors; naturally outgoing and confident infants are sometimes ready by the age of three; the shyer, less confident may not be ready until they are six or seven. The decision should be left to the parents advised by, for example, 'playschool' supervisors, grandparents or others whom they trust who have had ample opportunity to observe the child closely over time – and not forgetting the wishes of the child itself. Age itself should not be a consideration. Young children are immensely adaptable; their learning is not steady and linear, it goes in leaps and bounds with periods of apparently little change between. A child who does not begin reading until seven or eight can quickly catch and overtake one whose precocious reading began at three. Einstein didn't start speaking until he was about eight! This book has not been about pedagogy, but we are as strongly against the notion of forcing young children to attempt to read when they have no desire or interest as we are against forbidding them from reading when they clearly have an aptitude and are enjoying it, simply because of their age. Whatever the statistical averages might be, each child is *different* and variations from the statistical average can be astonishingly large – as they are in every other walk of life.

Once at school, children join different groups for different activities depending on their individual abilities and prowess at that stage in each activity. This means that they are likely to be in one group for reading, another for arithmetic, yet another for writing, for history, for philosophy, for religion and so on. This sounds like a logistical and organisational nightmare, and no doubt it will not be easy. It may be that there will be wide variations in the number of children in each class. However, there is no clear evidence that class size is a significant factor in learning despite the common assumption that smaller classes are always best. It may well be important in some areas of learning and not in others, but there appears to be no conclusive evidence at present. Much more important is the individuals' desires to learn which are strongly related to their interest and enjoyment. This will be much greater if they are in a group in which the learning is neither above their heads nor boringly easy. The organisational difficulty of this arrangement is a small price to pay if we are to teach each child according to his or her individual need. *We must no longer go on arranging teaching for the convenience of the institution.*

Schooling continues in this way right through to the age of fourteen. There is no primary and secondary school divide, simply school. Naturally, this will cause problems with infrastructure: where will the extra classrooms come from; what will we do with redundant secondary school buildings? Again, to argue thus is to put the institutional cart before the educational horse. In business, when new technology comes along, industries invest in new factories, plant and equipment or go out of business. There is pain and redundancy, but sooner or later, it has to be done – and the sooner the better. Besides, bricks and mortar can be adapted; the number of learners will not change, simply the way they learn.

Within the school curriculum, students will progress in each of the eighteen subjects suggested in Chapter Seven towards the School Leaving Certificate at the rates that best suit them as individuals. Each subject may be taken when the student is ready... history at the age of nine perhaps, but measurement not until thirteen. Once a subject is passed the student may choose either to carry on learning more, or to abandon the subject and use the time to spend on another more testing subject, or to take up a new subject that is outside the School Leaving Certificate altogether. For these non-curricular subjects, Accredited teachers (as distinct from School teachers) would be available to teach – much as young children today go to piano or dance lessons. Whether such teaching is carried on within school premises or not will depend on whatever is most practicable.

From the age of eleven – possibly earlier for some – each child will have access to a Mentor. Mentoring would be a separate profession from teaching: indeed, Mentors would not be able to be also Accredited teachers or School teachers. Their job, initially, is to find out directly from the child (i.e. not from the child's teachers or others) what his or her interests are, what they think they are good at and/or enjoy doing and, as a next step, to find out what things they've never tried and/or would like to try. Later these lines of questions can move into the realm of what they would like to become or to do for a living. Never should the answers be pooh-poohed. The Mentor asks the simple question "What do you think you need to learn (or practice) in order to increase your ability to achieve that goal?" If their chances of attaining their desires seem remote (or even if they don't), the questions should also explore what other possibilities the student would have as a fallback. In other words, the aspiring professional footballer might be asked "If you were to suffer a serious physical injury which precluded professional football, what else would you like to do?"

By the age of fourteen, all subjects of the School Leaving Certificate should have been passed. Any student who has not yet passed one or more subjects will be obliged to remain at school. Almost invariably these will be cases where remedial education is required or where there are special educational needs for those with unusual or difficult backgrounds (recent immigrants without English come to mind) or those with particular learning difficulties. These latter cases should, of course, have been identified long before fourteen and special provision accorded. The School Leaving Certificate curriculum and examinations must be designed to be passable by all (other than those that fall into such categories) by the age of fourteen at the latest. It should be the only state-wide public examination that anyone has to take. Any other examinations would be set by the organisation requiring a specific qualification for a specific purpose, either to enter it, to graduate within it or to be able to carry out a particular role or task.

Once the School Leaving Certificate is completed and the student has reached the age of fourteen then full Personal Education can begin. Probably with the help of a Mentor, subjects for learning that fall within each of the five broad categories outlined in Chapter Eight are selected and our student goes to Accredited teachers to pursue them. The five (six from age sixteen) broad areas are not there to restrict learning, but the reverse – to ensure that students do not restrict themselves to one or two single areas too early in their lives. As may be seen, many activities fall into more than one category. Team games such as football or cricket are both physical and involve teamwork and many of the Aesthetic/Cultural activities are also Creative. We believe that most young people have diverse interests. Those that do restrict themselves to as narrow a range of learning as they can are likely to have decided early what is their passion in life and to pursue it single-mindedly. The subject areas themselves may be followed in a number of ways. Some may be interested in painting, others in the history of art; some to learn to write as a novelist or a journalist, others to study literature. All will have access to a Mentor, if they wish, to guide them through the multiplicity of choices, to find the most suitable and accessible

Wot, No School?

Accredited teacher for each learning area. Since Accredited teachers will be paid by the hour per student they may work as long or as hard as they wish. Those who are most popular and good at their job will find most demand and *vice versa*.

Payment for students will be also based on the number of hours they work. Provided they are 'signed off' by an Accredited teacher on one hour minimum for each of the five (six at sixteen) broad subject areas per week, they will receive payment – and their parents will too. To prevent exploitation, we suggest a maximum of twenty five or thirty hours per week.

Visiting a number of different Accredited teachers does present logistical difficulties, and a travel subsidy system may be needed, especially in rural areas. We envisage that Accredited teachers will, in many cases, form associations amongst themselves as suggested in Chapter Eight, and may often occupy redundant school buildings where convenient. Indeed, there may well be cases where they occupy part of a building otherwise used as a school.

Signposts - Schools

1. Some far-reaching ideas were propounded in *One World One School*, the 'Vision 2020' July 2000 Conference Paper of the Technology Colleges Trust (now the Specialist Schools and Academies Trust). In the 'Futures Thinking' section of that paper the working party envisaged:

- *schools that are part private – part state funded;*

How schools impede education

- *all students with Individual Education Plans and, from the age of 14, considerable control over their own learning;*
- *para-teaching professionals, and business people working part-time.*

In their policy of 'Innovation and Abandonment' they foresaw

- *'pupils negotiating with their learning mentor… over the areas they want to specialise in';*
- *'learning time beyond the traditional six hour day, within and beyond the timetabled programme';*
- removing *'the distinction between academic and vocational education.'*

Working groups advocated the abandonment of *'School bells… Fixed days… Fixed lesson times…'* and a *'Fixed year… Teaching strategies which do not address the learning needs of disaffected students'* or *'do not enable sophisticated learners to gain challenging learning experiences'; 'assignments… which occupy time rather than enhance learning'* and *'Teaching restricted to classroom'.* As alternatives they proposed teaching *'key skills through work-related learning programmes… individual learning programmes with tutorial support… Focus on thinking skills, literacy and numeracy… A higher education teaching style Post-16'* and a curriculum which *'addresses the differing needs of pupils'.*

'We might not' they opined, *'in the future have school buildings as we have now'* and we should *'focus on individualised needs regardless of age'.* Much of this would mean *'reducing bureaucracy and simplifying systems',* the abandonment of the *'concept of full-time*

Wot, No School?

graduate recruitment to teaching' as well as *'One year university based teacher training'*. These would be replaced by *'Part-time portfolio teachers'* and the *'development of a new professionalism'*.

They further concluded that *'We have to find and articulate clearly the ethical and moral principles that form the basis for education and for our society'*; *'We need to accept that things don't have to be done the way they always have been done'*; and we should innovate by *'Focusing on the future, not just the present.'* Warming to their theme, they wrote – *'Abandon old hierarchies'*, recognise that *'Often, those in power have a vested interest in the status quo because they made it so,'* and that *'Habit is a deadener: tradition is slovenliness. You may always have done it that way but it doesn't work'*. Out go *'One track thinking... GCSEs... Traditional classrooms teaching in groups of 30...'* the *'Union approach'* and *'Rigid hierarchical structures'*. In their closing paragraphs they wrote: *'Some argue that we are going to see the end to schools, as we know. In looking to the future we should explore what this might mean and why'*.

They were clear that there was no longer a place for *'the factory school of the current century that was designed to meet very different needs'*.

What they were saying was that the old 'one-size fits all' curriculum, and by implication, 'one-size fits all' school itself, simply was not working. It needed to be changed to a system which put the needs of the learner first. They were proposing, as we are proposing, a system which considered education as more desirable than schooling and implied the closure of secondary schooling as we know it, though as secondary school teachers and Heads of secondary schools they could not say, possibly even yet see this. Subsequently, some of their schools have taken the first steps towards their vision but many of those attempts have been, like the other initiatives before theirs, throttled by the strangling chains of the institution itself.

2. As far back as 1990, Professor Charles Handy was suggesting the idea of 'Shamrock Schools'. By this he meant:

"The alternative is to think upside-down and turn the school into a shamrock with a core activity and everything else contracted out or done part-time by a flexible labour force. The core activity would be primarily one of educational manager, devising an appropriate educational programme for each child and arranging for its delivery. A core curriculum would continue to be taught directly by the school but anything outside the core would be contracted out to independent suppliers, new mini-schools. There might be a range of independent art schools, language schools, computing schools, design schools and others. These independent suppliers would be paid, by the core school, on a per capita basis, probably with an agreed minimum.

"The job of the school proper would be to set and monitor the standards of these mini-school outsiders, to ensure an adequate variety, to help students and their families decide on an educational programme from all that was available and to manage a core curriculum itself in order to maintain some sense of group cohesion at the centre.

"In this way, the school as a whole could be quite big because for most of the time the students would be in smaller mini-schools. The parents would choose, not so

Wot, No School?

much between schools as within schools, between the variety that was on offer. In big schools there could be a number of competing outside organisations offering courses in one particular area, such as art or language…

"Schools say that it will be more difficult to organise. The shamrock always is more difficult; but it does provide more flexibility, too. The student who is gifted at language school could progress faster, irrespective of age, even though the core groups in the school proper would still be year groups. Everybody progresses at different rates in different subject areas – the shamrock design makes it feasible to recognise this…. Of course the school day would have to change. The variety could not be programmed into the 35-minute slots beloved of school bureaucrats. The core curriculum could be taught on four mornings a week leaving the fifth day and every afternoon, and evening, for the mini-schools. There is, after all, no reason why every student has to finish school at the same time or could not learn to have a free afternoon followed by an early evening session in his or her design school. It is, come to think of it, more like the world of work they will be entering.

"The shamrock federal school could go even further. It could give each student their own … individual contract. In this contract there would be a core which the school would undertake to deliver and the individual to study. There would be an area of discretion, out of which the student could pick a range of options. There would be a clear definition of goals and measures of success … including the demonstration of capacities, such as interpersonal skills, practical competences and organising abilities which cannot be fully taught in classroom subjects. There would be planned opportunities to review and, if necessary, to revise the contract, on both sides.

How schools impede education

"The idea of an individual contract with each student … becomes much more plausible when the school has the flexibility of the shamrock and is really a federation of mini-schools. It would change the relationship between student and school making it one of partnership under contract and less one of teacher and child or warden and prisoner. School would be seen by more young people as a personal opportunity not a chore, they would be more like customers for some of the time, carrying a per capita income with them to the mini-schools they choose. Everybody might begin to take themselves and everybody else more seriously.

"Some of it is happening already. I telephoned a large community school, where adults study as well as teenagers and where activities go on until late into the evening. I asked to speak to the Head. 'Which Head?' said the receptionist, 'there are several heads of several schools here.' It was the outward sign of a federal shamrock."

The Age of Unreason Charles Handy (Arrow Books, 1990).

Many Secondary schools are forming 'federations' with others (though not in the form envisaged by Charles Handy) so that students have access to a much wider choice of subjects to study. We are simply advocating that this idea be taken to its logical conclusion and acknowledge that it is not the school that teaches you, it is the teacher.

3. A new qualification has recently been started by the government to run alongside A-levels. It is called the 14-19 Diploma. Lorna Unwin, professor of vocational education at London University Institute of Education

has described this qualification as 'an educational tease, masquerading as vocational qualifications when they are sufficiently academic to satisfy the needs of higher education'. She went on to say that 'Diplomas are a form of obese cuckoo in the education nest, stuffed full of academic requirements which will work hard to push out the more expensive and complex vocational component.' She called for the creation of centres for research and development in vocational practice which 'faced and uphill struggle for recognition… That prejudice is encapsulated in the terms "unskilled" and "low-skilled". They reflect the peculiar notion that many occupations are either completely devoid of or contain very little knowledge and technique and, therefore, the workers themselves are equally deficient. If we are dismissive of so many occupations it is not surprising that we are still struggling to build a well-functioning and respected system of vocational education.' [From: Unwin, L. (2009) *Sensuality, Sustainability and Social Justice: Vocational Education in Changing Times*, Inaugural Lecture, London: Institute of Education.] Readers may feel that they have read similar sentiments to these in Chapters Three and Four above.

4. If the previous paragraph reads like a case of one step forward and almost (or more than) one step back, it is also worth noting the experiment which is being developed at Bridgemary school in Gosport, which caters for pupils from 11 to 16, to allocate pupils to classes by ability rather than by age – our 'ladders' system in its infancy.

At Bridgemary, from September 2005, new arrivals with poor literacy or numeracy skills have been placed in primary school style groups with a single teacher for all their lessons. These pupils will progress at a rate suitable for them as individuals. They have been assessed and placed in groups for each subject. The new ability groups are called Access, Entry and Levels 1, 2 and 3. The plan could mean a 14-year-old will study history at Entry level but geography at Level 2. The head teacher explains the rationale: "Children are all different and we need to cater for their individual needs. If they are in a class beyond their capability then they become disaffected and do not want to learn. This can lead them to disrupt others. If youngsters get fed up in one subject then they may switch off in other lessons and lose interest in school. It is about personalising and recognising that children are all individuals and do not learn at the same pace." Today, the school (now Bridgemary Community Sports College) reports that the system is working extremely well. The first cohort of young people has now been right through the system and has achieved the best results in staff memory.

5. In 2009, two reports were published on Primary schools. Sir Jim Rose produced the Independent Review of the Primary Curriculum and had been commissioned by the government. It said some sensible, if excrutiatingly obvious things: for example, its aims were '…successful learners who enjoy learning, make progress and achieve; confident individuals able to lead safe, healthy and fulfilling lives; responsible citizens who make a positive contribution to society'. He proposed that there should be 'six areas of understanding: in English, communication and languages; maths; science and technology; human, social and environmental; physical health and wellbeing; the arts and design'. His core subjects would be 'literacy and numeracy, whilst making sure that serious attention is

Wot, No School?

paid to developing spoken language intensively…'
Almost simultaneously The Cambridge Primary Review
was published, the director of which was Robin
Alexander. This had the following aims: ' Wellbeing,
engagement, empowerment, autonomy, encouraging
respect and reciprocity, promoting interdependence and
sustainability, empowering local, national and global
citizenship, celebrating culture and community,
exploring, knowing, understanding and making sense,
fostering skill, exciting the imagination and enacting
dialogue.' The curriculum should have eight domains:
'arts and creativity, faith and belief, language, oracy and
literacy, mathematics, physical and emotional health,
place and time, science and technology. The core
curriculum is redefined as 'requirements for all the
specified domains, not just some, so "core" disappears.'

Readers may wish to compare these curriculum lists with
those given in Chapter Seven above. It is interesting that
Rose puts arts and design at the bottom of his list,
whereas Alexander puts arts and creativity at the top of
his.

6. An American headmaster of an English secondary
school started, in 2005, encouraging some of his pupils
to enrol on degree courses while still at school with the
Open University. The first three of these students have
now graduated. This initiative was so successful that
some 450 schools across Britain have since signed up
and about 4,000 young people are studying some of the
university's modules. Apparently education law had to
be altered to allow the university to offer this facility to
all schools. WHY? Do we need permission to be
educated now?

How schools impede education

Signposts – Further Education

In the current third tier of education, Further Education colleges are already well placed to interact with learning providers from outside the mainstream academic teaching profession, particularly with local employers whether small, medium or large. At present a growing number of 14-16 year olds - currently about 120000 of them - are already attending colleges of Further Education throughout the country for one or, sometimes, more days a week. At present these pupils are almost exclusively drawn from the ranks of those young people with whom schools are having the most difficulty; that is the regular truants, the excluded, those from difficult home backgrounds or who are in care and so on, or those who are considered especially 'gifted and talented' at things which their current schools cannot develop sufficiently. How much more could they do with the 40% or more of school pupils who currently struggle more or less manfully with an academic education in which they have little or no interest?

Sheffield College of Further Education, for instance, was in 2005 teaching about 1000 students in the 14-16 age range for one or two days a week. A small number of 'disaffected' students were attending full time. The scheme involved 14 local secondary schools, 7 sixth form colleges and 6 Special Schools. Central to the working of the scheme was the partnership with 'Sheffield Futures', the local 'Connexions' organisation originally set up to replace the various (and variable) careers guidance and advisory services provided in different LEAs, but soon emerging, in typical governmental bureaucratic fashion, as an organisation for 'less able' students only, i.e. as a cost cutting measure rather than an enhancement of the existing services.

Significantly, private Training Providers (linked with local employers) are very important to the scheme. The college and groups of schools in strategic locations of the city are currently looking at developing common timetable arrangements so that students can attend courses not only at the college, but also at other schools if they are better placed to provide the course (e.g. specialist language or ICT).

Though a minority of students are not even at entry level (e.g. cannot fill in an application form) for the most part students are increasingly doing qualifications at levels 1 and 2. There is also a positive 'knock on' effect on students' school work from spending one or two days a week at college. In college they are offered what they believe to be more motivating and relevant learning opportunities and are treated more as adults than they believe they are in school. Many of the lecturers are embracing the 14-19 ethos for the benefit of the young people and once students see some success in one area, they are much more likely to start achieving it in others.

In another example, City College Brighton and Hove provides places for about 350 14-16 year olds on courses that range across the curriculum including catering, construction, engineering, manufacturing, retail business and hairdressing. They arrange individual programmes for a small number of students for whom full-time education is not appropriate because of exclusion, difficult home situations or who are in care. They also cater, interestingly, for a few independent school dropouts.

How schools impede education

As a final example of another pointer towards the system we propose, Great Yarmouth College of Further Education has been involved in providing education for 14-16 year olds for some 15 years, and working with three or four local High Schools. Now, under the Achievement Education Action Zone and the Increasing Flexibility Programme, eight schools are involved and around nine hundred 14-16 year olds attend Great Yarmouth College for between two and four hours per week. The 14-16 year olds spend two days per week at school doing core subjects, half a day at the college, one day work placement and one day with Skill Force – an independent organisation originally sponsored by the Ministry of Defence and using ex MoD personnel – who work on improving self-esteem, team skills and interpersonal skills towards Award Scheme Development and Accreditation Network (ASDAN) qualifications. At present, all these students work towards National Vocational Qualifications, which some at the college believe are totally unsuitable for this age group.

Signposts – Skill Force

Skill Force UK Ltd. provides skill development training primarily for 14-16 year olds during the school working week. There are, at the time of writing, thirty two teams, staffed mainly but not exclusively by former armed services personnel, operating throughout the UK, working with over nine thousand five hundred young people from 200 schools attending courses. Skill Force's aim is eventually to become predominantly self-funded by the participating schools. The young people are not just those who find academic subjects difficult but some who are classed as 'gifted and talented'. There are also specialised courses for some who fall outside this age range.

Most of the training is still classroom based though there are organised outdoor activities. These tend to attract attention from a tabloid press which, quite wrongly, labels them 'boot camps', as though they were for disciplinary rather than educational purposes. Manifestly they are not, though for many in the media what Skill Force do may be so far removed from their own personal educational experience that it is difficult to understand - and makes, anyway, a far less exciting and inflammatory story. Among the skills taught are team-working, problem solving, planning and reviewing team-based exercises, job seeking and interviewee skills.

The main benefit of the training, apart from the specific skills development is that the young people involved – many of whom have had little or no success in academic work at school – gain a strong sense of achievement and the awareness that they can succeed at non-school activities and that they do possess valuable and valued skills and potential.

A review of their work was carried out by the Institute of Education, (*Evaluation of Skill Force* – Institute of Education, University of London, October 2003). As being among those who have not only studied this report but also visited Skill Force in action, we would strongly recommend it to anyone who needs to believe that there are the seeds here not only of a future for the extraordinarily fortunate children who participate in this programme, but for all young people in this country – as soon as we remove the academic shackles of a wasted and wasteful schooling system.

Questions

The aim of this book is to create a debate about education that looks beyond the mighty structures and institutions created by the School Industry. We have, we hope, drawn a picture – perhaps a rough sketch of how young people should be educated in a way that reconciles as far as possible the needs of society as it is today with the very personal needs of each individual to grow in the way that is best for them rather than what is best for institutions and politicians. We do not pretend to have all the answers on how this is to be achieved. We believe that if the will is there the means will be found. Here then is a short list of questions for which we would like you to supply the answers:

1. Accredited Teachers. We believe that these people should be drawn from as wide a range as possible – age, work experience, specialist knowledge and skills, life experience whose common interest is in the development of the potential in all young people. Beyond the obvious Child Protection legal requirement, how can they become Accredited? Should there be some sort of exam? Should they serve some sort of 'teaching apprenticeship'? In our view, the answers should be unbureaucratic and set very low academic barriers – or none at all.

2. Testing and Examination. Our own preference would be that there should no public tests or examinations other than the School Leaving Certificate. All other tests

should be set by the bodies that require particular skills or qualifications. This could well mean that universities, for example, create a common University Entrance Exam which could be not dissimilar from the current A-level or International Baccalaureate exams. However, we recognise that there could be a demand for some sort of general test for students who are not pursuing an entirely work or higher education learning path. We believe that their 'Log Book' of learning should be sufficient, but others may not agree. Perhaps the ASDAN (Award Scheme Development and Accreditation Network) programme could be the answer here. What do you think?

3. Pay for Accredited Teachers, Students and Parents. How much should it be and how should it be paid? Our suggestion is that students'/parents' pay should be related to the National Minimum Wage: something like £4 per hour split 50/50 between parent and student for 14-16 year olds and £5 per hour for 16+. Accredited Teachers could receive similar amounts per hour per pupil. Thus teaching an average of 10 students for 20 hours per week would bring in £800 to £1000 per week. This is not a king's ransom, but nor is it a pittance.

4. The School Leaving Certificate Examinations. In Chapter Seven, we listed eighteen subject areas for the School Leaving Certificate. We do not pretend to be experts in all these subject areas (!) and would welcome your amplification of what the curricula contents should be for each. Are there other vital subject areas we have overlooked? Should there be flexibility? What level of knowledge or understanding should be required in each? Should targets or guidelines be set against averages etc.? (We believe not, given that these would inevitably lead

How schools impede education

to league tables, institutional competitiveness and so on – the very things that are ruining so many young peoples' lives today.)

5. Pick-and-Mix Learning. There is a danger that some young people will spend the four years of their Personal Education switching frequently from one subject area to another more or less at random. Young people might be tempted to 'play around' with 'softer' options and rather than tackle the rigorous learning regime required for, say, entrance to a medical school. We don't believe that this will be a major problem though there will doubtless be sad cases. Students who have an aptitude for academic work will have every opportunity to pursue their goals with appropriate Accredited teachers and be paid to do it. Access to dedicated Mentors will help them gradually bring their interests and talents into focus and, if they have taken an unsuitable path, help them to find another. We believe that young people will leap at the chance to fashion their own future through learning and that the major problem will be adults fearful of losing control. However, we would welcome your views on this undoubtedly interesting, not to say tricky, area.

This is not a comprehensive list and your views on any other question raised by our proposals will happily be aired and debated. Please email debate@wotnoschool.com to join the debate.

The Purpose of this Book

The purpose of this book is to start a debate about the *real* problem of how we should educate our young people. To be winners today, young people have to be 'good at school' (or very lucky). A great many of them – about half – aren't 'good at school' and are thus classed as failures before life has properly begun.

We believe that *all* are good at *something*.

The great barrier to education for teachers and learners is the system; the institution of school itself (especially post fourteen) and the ludicrous insistence that *academic ability is the greatest good* for all young people. This strange notion is based on nothing more than the fact that schools have *always* taught academic subjects and learners have *always* been measured by their academic ability. Those who are successful at this go on, in their time, to control the institutional school industry – and what was good enough for them...

Now we measure the 'performance of schools' (as if inanimate institutions can 'perform') so that teachers and heads can be rewarded or castigated and the institution treated like a manufacturing production line processing identical raw materials and trying to produce identical 'outputs'. Schools and the industry that controls them – from government to quangos to local authorities to Ofsted and now to something new to control 'academies' – have become more important than the unique individual human beings that they try to process.

How schools impede education

No one has stopped to ask 'What is education *for*?' Instead, they go on measuring the measurable – academic attainments – and ignoring the nurture of non-academic abilities and of what cannot be measured: independence of thought, originality and creativity, sociability, willingness to co-operate with others, a 'can do' autonomous approach to life and so on. These are the very birthright of every young person regardless of her or his academic ability.

This book reveals how modern Britain arrived at this present fixation with academic success and proposes a radical approach to the business of educating our young people to ensure that *all* will have the opportunity both to take a full and positive part in adult life and to develop their own peculiar and particular sets of aptitudes and abilities.

Join the debate by visiting www.wotnoschool.com the website that is dedicated to debating the issues addressed in this book.